DR. DAVID JEREMIAH

TEN STEPS TO
SPIRITUAL
RENEWAL

The Book of Nehemiah

STUDY GUIDE

with Dr. David Jeremiah

Edited by William Kruidenier

Unless otherwise indicated, Scripture verses quoted are taken from the NEW KING JAMES VERSION.

Printed in the United States of America.

CONTENTS

ABOUT DR. DAVID JEREMIAH AND TURNING POINT

D
r. David Jeremiah is the founder of Turning Point, a ministry committed to providing Christians with sound Bible teaching relevant to today's changing times through radio and television broadcasts, audio series, books, and live events. Dr. Jeremiah's common-sense teaching on topics such as family, prayer, worship, angels, and biblical prophecy forms the foundation of Turning Point.

David and his wife, Donna, reside in El Cajon, California, where he serves as the senior pastor of Shadow Mountain Community Church. David and Donna have four children and twelve grandchildren.

In 1982, Dr. Jeremiah brought the same solid teaching to San Diego television that he shares weekly with his congregation. Shortly thereafter, Turning Point expanded its ministry to radio. Dr. Jeremiah's inspiring messages can now be heard worldwide on radio, television, and the Internet.

Because Dr. Jeremiah desires to know his listening audience, he travels nationwide holding ministry rallies and spiritual enrichment conferences that touch the hearts and lives of many people. According to Dr. Jeremiah, "At some point in time, everyone reaches a turning point; and for every person, that moment is unique, an experience to hold onto forever. There's so much changing in today's world that sometimes it's difficult to choose the right path. Turning Point offers people an understanding of God's Word as well as the opportunity to make a difference in their lives."

Dr. Jeremiah has authored numerous books, including *Escape the Coming Night* (Revelation), *The Handwriting on the Wall* (Daniel), *Overcoming Loneliness, Prayer—The Great Adventure, Captured by Grace, Signs of Life, Agents of the Apocalypse, Agents of Babylon, A Life Beyond Amazing, Forward, Everything You Need, Shelter in God, The Jesus You May Not Know* and *The God You May Not Know.*

HOW TO USE THIS STUDY GUIDE

The purpose of this Turning Point study guide is to reinforce Dr. David Jeremiah's dynamic, in-depth teaching and to aid the reader in applying biblical truth to his or her daily life. This study guide is designed to be used in conjunction with Dr. Jeremiah's *Ten Steps to Spiritual Renewal* audio series, but it may also be used by itself for personal or group study.

STRUCTURE OF THE LESSONS

Each lesson is based on one of the messages in the *Ten Steps to Spiritual Renewal* compact disc series and focuses on specific passages in the Bible. Each lesson is composed of the following elements:

- *Outline*

The outline at the beginning of the lesson gives a clear, concise picture of the topic being studied and provides a helpful framework for readers as they listen to Dr. Jeremiah's teaching.

- *Overview*

The overview summarizes Dr. Jeremiah's teaching on the passage being studied in the lesson. Readers should refer to the Scripture passages in their own Bibles as they study the overview. Unless otherwise indicated, Scripture verses quoted are taken from the New King James Version.

- *Personal and Group Application Questions*

This section contains a variety of questions designed to help readers dig deeper into the lesson and the Scriptures, and to apply the lesson to their daily lives. For Bible study groups or Sunday school classes, these questions will provide a springboard for group discussion and interaction.

- *Did You Know?*

This section presents a fascinating fact, historical note, or insight that adds a point of interest to the preceding lesson.

PERSONAL STUDY

Thank you for selecting *Ten Steps to Spiritual Renewal* for your current study. The lessons in this study guide were created to help you gain fresh insights into God's Word and develop new perspectives on topics you may have previously studied. Each lesson is designed to challenge your thinking, and help you grow in your knowledge of Christ. During your study, it is our prayer that you will discover how biblical truth affects every aspect of your life and your relationship with Christ will be strengthened.

When you commit to completing this study guide, try to set apart a time, daily or weekly, to read through the lessons without distraction. Have your Bible nearby when you read the study guide, so you're ready to look up verses if you need to. If you want to use a notebook to write down your thoughts, be sure to have that handy as well. Take your time to think through and answer the questions. If you plan on reading the study guide with a small group, be sure to read ahead and be prepared to take part in the weekly discussions.

LEADER'S GUIDE

Thank you for your commitment to lead a group through *Ten Steps to Spiritual Renewal*. Being a leader has its own rewards. You may discover that your walk with the Lord deepens through this experience. Throughout the study guide, your group will explore new topics and review study questions that encourage thought-provoking group discussion.

The lessons in this study guide are suitable for Sunday school classes, small-group studies, elective Bible studies, or home Bible study groups. Each lesson is structured to provoke thought and help you grow in your knowledge and understanding of God. There are multiple components in this section that can help you structure your lessons and discussion time, so make sure you read and consider each one.

Before You Begin

Before you begin each meeting, make sure you and your group are well-versed with the content of the chapter. Every person should have his or her own study guide so they can follow along and write in the study guide if need be. When possible, the study guide should be used with the corresponding compact disc series. You may wish to assign the study guide lesson as homework prior to the meeting of the group and then use the meeting time to listen to the CD and discuss the lesson.

To ensure that everyone has a chance to participate in the discussion, the ideal size for a group is around eight to ten people. If there are more than ten people, try to break up the bigger group into smaller subgroups. Make sure the members are committed to participating each week, as this will help create stability and help you better prepare the structure of the meeting.

At the beginning of the study each week, start the session with a question to challenge group members to think about the issues you will be discussing. The members can answer briefly, but the goal is to have an idea in their mind as you go over the lesson. This allows the group members to become engaged and ready to interact with the group.

After reviewing the lesson, try to initiate a free-flowing discussion. Invite group members to bring questions and insights they may have discovered to the next meeting, especially if they were unsure of the meaning of some parts of the lesson. Be prepared to discuss how biblical truth applies to the world we live in today.

Weekly Preparation

As the group leader, here are a few things you can do to prepare for each meeting:

- Choose whether or not you will play the CD message during your small group session.

  If you decide to play the CD message from Dr. Jeremiah as part of the meeting, you will need to adjust the group time accordingly.

- Make sure you are thoroughly familiar with the material in the lesson.

  Make sure you understand the content of the lesson so you know how to structure group time and you are prepared to lead group discussion.

- Decide, ahead of time, which questions you plan to discuss.

  Depending on how much time you have each week, you may not be able to reflect on every question. Select specific questions which you feel will evoke the best discussion.

- Take prayer requests.

  At the end of your discussion, take prayer requests from your group members and pray for each other.

Structuring the Discussion Time

If you need help in organizing your time when planning your group Bible study, here are two schedules, for sixty minutes and ninety minutes, which can give you a structure for the lesson:

Option 1 (Listen to Audio CD)	60 Minutes	90 Minutes
Welcome: Members arrive and get settled.	N/A	5 minutes
Getting Started Question: Prepares the group for interacting with one another.	Welcome and Getting Started 5 minutes	15 minutes
Message: Listen to the audio CD.	40 minutes	40 minutes
Discussion: Discuss group study questions.	10 minutes	25 minutes
Prayer and Application: Final application for the week and prayer before dismissal.	5 minutes	5 minutes

Option 2 (No Audio CD)	60 Minutes	90 Minutes
Welcome: Members arrive and get settled.	5 minutes	10 minutes
Getting Started Question: Prepares the group for interacting with one another.	10 minutes	10 minutes
Message: Review the lesson.	15 minutes	25 minutes
Discussion: Discuss group study questions.	25 minutes	35 minutes
Prayer and Application: Final application for the week and prayer before dismissal.	5 minutes	10 minutes

As the group leader, it is up to you to keep track of the time and keep things moving along according to your schedule. If your group is having a good discussion, don't feel the need to stop and move on to the next question. Remember, the purpose is to pull together ideas, and share unique insights on the lesson. Make time each week to discuss how to apply these truths to living for Christ today.

The purpose of discussion is for everyone to participate, but don't be concerned if certain group members are more quiet—they may be internally reflecting on the questions and need time to process their ideas before they can share them.

Group Dynamics

Leading a group study can be a rewarding experience for you and your group members—but that doesn't mean there won't be challenges. Certain members may feel uncomfortable discussing topics that they consider very personal, and might be afraid of being called on. Some members might have disagreements on specific issues. To help prevent these scenarios, consider the following ground rules:

- If someone has a question that may seem off topic, suggest that it is discussed at another time, or ask the group if they are okay with addressing that topic.

- If someone asks a question you don't know the answer to, confess that you don't know and move on. If you feel comfortable, invite other group members to give their opinions, or share their comments based on personal experience.

- If you feel like a couple of people are talking much more than others, direct questions to people who may not have shared yet. You could even ask the more dominating members to help draw out the quiet ones.

- When there is a disagreement, encourage the group members to process the matter in love. Invite members from opposing sides to evaluate their opinions and consider the ideas of the other members. Lead the group through Scripture that addresses the topic, and look for common ground.

When issues arise, remind your group to think of Scripture: "Love one another" (John 13:34), "If it is possible, as much as depends on you, live peaceably with all men" (Romans 12:18), and "Be quick to listen, slow to speak and slow to become angry" (James 1:19, NIV).

FOR CONTINUING STUDY

For a complete listing of Dr. Jeremiah's materials for personal and group study call 1-800-947-1993, go online to www.DavidJeremiah.org, or write to Turning Point, P.O. Box 3838, San Diego, CA 92163.

Dr. Jeremiah's *Turning Point* program is currently heard or viewed around the world on radio, television, and the Internet in English. *Momento Decisivo*, the Spanish translation of Dr. Jeremiah's messages, can be heard on radio in every Spanish speaking country in the world. The television broadcast is also broadcast by satellite throughout the Middle East with Arabic subtitles.

Contact Turning Point for radio and television program times and stations in your area, or visit our website at www.DavidJeremiah.org/stationlocator.

TEN STEPS TO SPIRITUAL RENEWAL

INTRODUCTION

More than one thousand miles from where you live is the city of your forefathers. You know it only by accounts of its former glory. You were born in a foreign land where your people have been held captive for seventy years. You learn that the ancient city lies in ruins. The walls are broken down, the gates are burned, and it is home only to the poor and displaced who have made a living amidst its ruins.

You have in your mind the image of its former beauty and glory, but the picture you now imagine haunts you day and night. Somehow you believe that God wants you to return to the city—His city—to rebuild its walls and provide safety for its people.

But how? You are the captive servant of the most powerful king in the world who owns the very air you breath. What possible hope is there that he will allow you to leave his service and return to a city to rebuild the walls that protect a temple in which a God is worshiped at whom he scoffs? What hope, indeed!

So you take your burden to the God of your fathers and ask Him to make a way. You pray, and you wait. Four months after hearing the news about the city, on a day when the burden of its ruins weighs heavily on your heart, the king asks the reason for your fallen countenance. After you explain that the city of your fathers lies in ruin, the hand of God becomes clear: The king grants you a leave of absence to return and rebuild the walls around the city!

He gives you letters of passage and the resources you need and the walls are miraculously completed in 52 days. But then you realize that the walls are not the only source of protection that needs rebuilding. The spiritual defenses of the people of the city are every bit as weak as the walls; there is as much rubble covering their hearts as there was covering the foundations of city walls. If the city of your fathers—the city of your fathers' God—is to live again, more than walls of stone must be rebuilt. Walls of faith and obedience must be rebuilt in the hearts of the people.

Now that the people are safe behind solid walls and gates, the harder job begins: challenging the people to renew their covenant with God.

That was the challenge faced by one of the most remarkable men in the Bible: Nehemiah. Cupbearer to the king of Persia, he returned to Jerusalem to convince a disheartened, faithless remnant of Jewish refugees that the God of Abraham, Isaac, and Jacob wanted to be their God as well; to convince them to renew their faith and rebuild their understanding of what it meant to walk in covenant with the God who chose them to be the most unique people in all the earth.

At that unlikely task, Nehemiah was successful. Just as God made a way for him to return to Jerusalem, He made a way for him and his coworker Ezra to lead the people of Jerusalem to renew their faith. Nehemiah set out ten goals for the Jewish remnant that needed to be met if they were to experience the blessings God had waiting for them—and they reached all ten.

By following Nehemiah's *Ten Steps to Spiritual Renewal,* any follower of Jesus Christ can restore his or her faith. Like building a wall, stones of faith are laid one at a time. But when complete, such a renewed faith can withstand the strongest assault of any enemy.

Step Number 1:

GETTING BACK TO THE BOOK

Nehemiah 8:1-12

In this lesson we learn why obedience to Scripture is the foundation for spiritual renewal.

OUTLINE

All Christians profess to wanting to grow spiritually—to become known as a "mature" believer in Christ. But not all Christians are equally eager to do what is required to reach that goal. An unswerving commitment to the authority of Scripture—knowing and obeying the Bible—is key.

I. How the People Prepared to Hear the Word of God
  A. They Asked for the Word of God
  B. They Came Together as One Man
  C. They Stayed for Hours
  D. They Stood Up
  E. They Gave Attention

II. How the Word of God Was Presented
  A. From the Pulpit
  B. In the Sight of All the People
  C. In a Certain Way

III. The Three Things That Happened as a Result
  A. They Worshiped
  B. They Wept
  C. They Went

In 1742, John Albert Bingle observed that Scripture is the foundation of the Church and the Church is the guardian of Scripture. Nothing has changed—that relationship between Scripture and the Church remains true today.

The true spiritual health of any church can be directly correlated with how that church views and handles the Bible. Either the church will be nourished and made healthy as a result of attention to the Word of God, or the Word will languish, untouched, in the corner of a church that is having no impact for Christ. Churches that feed on the Word of God are healthy and vibrant, while churches that exist on a diet of spiritual "junk food" are weak and malnourished. Sadly, there are many of these weak churches in existence today.

In Nehemiah's day, when the Jewish remnant returned from captivity in Babylon to Jerusalem, the Word of God was the center of the peoples' spiritual strength. If the Church today is ever going to experience the revival that Israel experienced under Ezra and Nehemiah, it will be because of allegiance and obedience to the Word of God.

I heard a great Bible teacher, Dr. John Whitcomb, say at a conference many years ago something I have never forgotten. He said that Satan used liberalism in the early twentieth century to try to take the Word of God away from the Church—but he failed. Since that didn't work, Satan's next strategy would be to try to take the Church away from the Word. And in that he has had greater success.

Christianity in America has become dangerously centered on experience instead of the truth of Scripture. When we set aside the Word and focus on what we have experienced, we will eventually lose our way. Spiritual renewal and maturity come only when we make God's Word the priority—our only rule for faith and practice. The ancient prophecy of Amos 8:11 might well be applied to the modern Church: "I will send a famine on the land, not a famine of bread, nor a thirst for water, but of hearing the words of the Lord."

I sometimes am met with incredulous looks by other church leaders when they find out that teaching the Word is the focus at the church I pastor. Yes, we have plenty of wonderful worship and other varied forms of ministry during our services. But they have not been allowed to replace the prominent role of instruction from the Bible. And in the book of Nehemiah, we will find that the people were asked to recognize Scripture in the same way: the center of their spiritual renewal.

By the end of Nehemiah 7, something is wrong in Jerusalem: The Word of God has not been made the center of the spiritual community. The people were rebuilding their city, but they were not rebuilding their hearts. In the thirteen years the people had been back in Jerusalem there is no mention of the centrality of Scripture —until we get to Nehemiah 8.

HOW THE PEOPLE PREPARED TO HEAR THE WORD OF GOD

Beginning in Nehemiah 8:1, we find that "all the people gathered together as one man" in Jerusalem. All the people—"men and women" (verse 2) came together in unity to hear the Word of God. And in verse 4 we are given the names of the leaders who stood on Ezra's right and left on the platform created for the reading of the Word. Even some children gathered with their parents. They were included in the "all who could hear with understanding" (verse 2). Adults, children, leaders—all were there to hear the reading of Scripture. The most interesting insight of all is that it was the people who "told Ezra the scribe to bring the Book of the Law of Moses" and read to them (verse 1).

They Asked for the Word of God

The people calling for the Word of God reminds me of times I've preached in countries like Romania and Ecuador. The people will stay up all night to hear the Word—and then ask you to teach them more! Sadly, we don't find this hunger so much in developed countries where the Church takes the Word of God for granted.

They Came Together as One Man

The reference to coming together as "one man" refers to their unity. There was a consensus among the people that they had been ignoring God's truth.

They Stayed for Hours

Ezra read "from morning until midday" (verse 3)—so roughly three to four hours. This was no casual commitment, especially since they were standing the entire time.

They Stood Up

When Ezra opened the Book of the Law of Moses, "all the people stood up" (verse 5). And there is no mention of them sitting down. Standing is an act of honor; sitting is an act of relaxation or resting. The people in Jerusalem that day honored the Scriptures with their body language.

They Gave Attention

Verse 3 says the people "were attentive to the Book of the Law." They didn't have notebooks or Bibles to make notes in like we do, but they were attentive nonetheless. Their attitude was, "I want to hear; I want to learn; I want to receive what God is saying through His Word."

It's easy today to become critical in church—critical of the preacher, the music, the temperature in the room, or the color of the choir robes. When that happens we completely lose sight of the Word. I remember during our seminary training that my wife and I came to the conclusion that there is something in every single church service to get excited about—if we will look for it! The preacher and musicians can only do so much. We have to show up with an attitude of expectation and attention, just like the people in Jerusalem that day. The pattern, once prominent in our culture, of Christians preparing themselves on Saturday night for church on Sunday, has been mostly lost. It may be one reason believers are disappointed with church.

HOW THE WORD OF GOD WAS PRESENTED

Verses 4-8 detail how Ezra went about presenting the Word to the people.

From the Pulpit

A "platform of wood" (verse 4) was built for Ezra and the other leaders, roughly parallel to a modern-day pulpit in terms of purpose if not design. In fact, the King James Version of the Bible calls it a "pulpit" rather than a platform—but platform is the better translation. The platform was made "for the purpose" (verse 4) of giving honor to the Word of God; a place to draw the focus of the gathered congregation. It represents the central place of the Word in the life of God's people.

In the Sight of All the People

There was only one copy of the Book of the Law. Ezra did not say, "Please take your Bibles and turn to page . . . ." The Word of God was positioned "in the sight of all the people" (verse 5) so they might hear and see clearly.

In a Certain Way

Verse 8 is the most important verse in this passage because it provides a model for communicating the Word of God: "So they read distinctly from the book, in the Law of God; and they gave the sense, and helped them to understand the reading."

As best I can tell, Ezra would read a portion, then give "the sense"—explain to the people what Moses had written. It is said that the great Charles Spurgeon followed this same practice, basically delivering a small sermon via the Scripture reading and relevant comments before giving his actual sermon later. This "pre-sermon" gave the congregation a sense of the passage on which he would later preach, preparing them ahead of time.

There is a sense in which the scarcity of copies of the Bible in ancient and medieval times resulted in more forced and focused concentration. Today, there are so many Bibles available that we tend to treat it as just another book, not giving it the honor it deserves. When there is only one copy and one translation, no one takes it for granted.

Giving "the sense" of a passage involves three things (at least this is what I pray for my own preaching ministry): seeing what the text says (observation); seeing what it meant in its original context (interpretation); and understanding what it means to today's audience (application). Without the final step of application, the message is not complete. The Bible is not just a book of history. It is a living book given to change the lives of those who read it. There is no question that change was Ezra's goal. He wanted the returned remnant from Babylon to be different from the generation that had been exiled as a result of ignoring God's Word. Teaching must result in change. Teaching is not talking; it is communicating so lives are changed.

THE THREE THINGS THAT HAPPENED AS A RESULT

Even though the people of Israel had accomplished a lot by rebuilding the walls of the city, something was still missing in their experience. As a result of asking Ezra to read the Book of the Law to them, three things happened.

They Worshiped

Go through the rest of this passage to the end of chapter 8 and note the action verbs. When the Word of God is proclaimed faithfully and accurately, action is the result. In fact, even before Ezra began to read, as a result of his blessing the Lord, "the people answered, 'Amen, Amen!' while lifting up their hands. And they bowed their heads and worshiped the Lord with their faces to the ground" (verse 6).

And then when Ezra read about the Feast of Tabernacles, they realized they had been negligent in keeping that feast—so they immediately set about to correct that omission. Preaching followed by worship and action is the biblical pattern, something we might want to consider implementing in the modern church. Most contemporary churches place worship first in their order of service as a means of expressing the priority of worship. While there is nothing unbiblical about that practice, there is certainly precedence for worship coming after the preaching of the Word as a means of response.

They Wept

When the people heard the Word of God, they wept (verse 9)! There is no question they fell under conviction due to their failure to live according to its precepts. This should not be an unusual or unnatural response. In today's world, especially with men, showing emotion over the things of God is rarely seen. It is considered to be a sign of weakness, or a lack of sophistication in spiritual matters. Yet, if we truly hear and understand the Word of God, how can we not be convicted by it? There is no doubt that the Israelites felt great remorse, shame, and guilt over the years they had spent in captivity as a result of their fathers and forefathers failing to obey God's Word.

First Samuel 3:1 reveals an attitude that we ought to find in our own hearts about the Word of God: "And the word of the Lord was rare in those days; there was no widespread revelation." What is the law of supply and demand? When things are scarce, they go up in value; they become precious to us. The people had been without the Word for so long that they began to weep when they heard it, tears of joy mixed with tears of shame.

They Went

Now we see a series of action words: Nehemiah told the people to *go, eat, drink,* and *send* food to others (verse 10). Instead of standing there weeping in their guilt and humiliation, they were commanded to go and celebrate the goodness of the Lord. And that is always the litmus test of how we have received the Word of God. Do we allow it to convict us so that we remain under its judgment, or do we rise up in the forgiving freedom God offers and live out its instructions? Obviously, Ezra and Nehemiah wanted the people to do the latter.

The immediate way to put the Word into action was to carry out the instructions regarding the Feast of Tabernacles (also called the Feast of Booths) (verses 13-18). Verse 17 suggests that this Feast had been ignored in Israel since the days of Joshua—quite a long time!

The Feast of Tabernacles was to be celebrated in the seventh month of the year (our September to October) for two reasons. First, the booths that the people constructed and dwelt in for seven days memorialized the temporary dwellings the Hebrew slaves lived in on the journey from Egypt to Canaan. Second, it was to celebrate the goodness of God for bringing them into the Promised Land and giving them an abundant harvest. One commentator I read called it an "ecclesiastical campout"—a time to remember when things were tenuous in their lives, creating in them a sense of gratitude for all God had given them.

It would have been easy for them to think, "Surely if this feast has not been kept since Joshua's day, there is no requirement for us to keep it now." Instead, they were of a mind to do whatever the Word of God said. The Word said to build booths, or temporary huts, out of branches and leaves—so that's what they did. They didn't debate the relevance, importance, or practicality of the instructions. They just did what the Word of God said for them to do as a way of demonstrating a desire to please God and live with His blessing instead of His judgment.

There can be no spiritual renewal in anyone's life without a commitment to obeying the Word of God. If we want God's blessing, we have to live with the attitude expressed in the words of Christ Himself: "But why do you call Me 'Lord, Lord,' and not do the things which I say?" (Luke 6:46) To pray, "Lord, bless Your people," when the people are routinely treating as optional the things He has said is a contradictory notion. We have to approach the Word of God as a book full of precepts and instructions that are not only for God's glory but for our good as well. We have to approach the Word with a sense of expectancy about what we will discover when we read it: "Open my eyes, that I may see wondrous things from Your law" (Psalm 119:18).

Is that your sense as you begin this study guide? The first step toward spiritual maturity for any follower of Jesus is to get back to the Book. It is there that we will discover the will of God—those fundamentals that must characterize the life of every Christian. Without knowing and obeying them, there can be no further progress toward maturity.

1. Read Hebrews 4:11-12.

   a. What do you learn from verse 12 about why the Bible is different from other books?

   b. What does "living and powerful" mean? How is the Bible alive?

   c. Why does verse 12 follow the warning in verse 11? What is the connection?

2. Read Nehemiah 8.

   a. Who gathered together to hear Ezra read from the Book of the Law of Moses? (verses 1-2)

b. For how long did the people gather in front of the Water Gate to hear the Word? (verse 3)

c. In verse 5, how did the people show their attentiveness to Ezra while he read?

d. In what three ways did the crowd respond according to verses 6, 9, and 10?

e. What did Nehemiah command the people to do in verse 10?

f. What words of the law did the people obey immediately after hearing them? (verses 13-18)

g. How long had the people of Israel ignored the Feast of Tabernacles?

h. What did the peoples' obedience demonstrate?

3. Read Psalm 119:18.

   a. What does this verse say about expectancy with regard to God's Word?

   b. How would you measure your own desire for God's Word?

   c. What one action can you take this week to grow in desire for the Word of God?

1. Read Nehemiah 8 as a group.

   a. Who assembled to hear Ezra read the Book of the Law of Moses? (verse 2)

   b. How did the people honor God's Word with their body language as Ezra read? (verse 5)

   c. According to verses 4-5, how did Ezra and the other leaders present the Word of God to the crowd?

   d. Discuss whether or not the Church today treats God's Word with the same respect that Ezra and the people did.

   e. What did the crowd shout while lifting their hands in verse 6? Was their reaction to the Word positive or negative? Compare and contrast their reaction to peoples' reaction to the reading of Scripture today.

f. What was the reaction of the people as they were convicted by the Word of God? (verse 9)

g. Why should we respond the same way the people of Israel did when the Bible convicts us of our sin?

h. For what two reasons was the Feast of Tabernacles celebrated in the seventh month of the year?

2. Read Luke 6:46 together.

a. Why should we live with the attitude expressed in this verse?

b. In what way(s) are we to approach God's Word in our own lives?

3. Share with the group one action you are planning to take to grow in your desire for God's Word.

DID YOU KNOW?

I n most modern, non-liturgical Protestant churches today, the pulpit is placed in the center of the church to emphasize the central importance of the proclamation of the Word of God in the worship service. Other churches (Catholic, Episcopal, and other liturgical denominations) place the altar in the center of the sanctuary with the pulpit to the side. This has its roots in the Roman Catholic tradition of the Mass taking precedence over everything else in the worship service. Some liturgical traditions have kept the altar (for example, the Anglican tradition) in its central place while distancing themselves from the Catholic view of sacrifice associated with the Mass.

Step Number 2:

GETTING SERIOUS ABOUT OBEDIENCE

Nehemiah 8:13-18

In this lesson we discover five dynamics related to obedience in the Christian life.

OUTLINE

The Bible is like no other book in world literature. One portion of the Bible even promises a blessing to those who read and take to heart what is written in it (Revelation 1:3). "Taking to heart" the Bible is another way of describing obedience. Reading is good, but obeying is better.

I. Obedience Is Related to Hunger

II. Obedience Is Related to Humility

III. Obedience Is Related to Honesty

IV. Obedience Is Related to Habit

V. Obedience Is Related to Happiness

I n the previous lesson we saw that the centrality of the Word of God is step number one toward spiritual renewal and maturity. But merely reading the Bible is not enough. There are many people who know the Bible well who are not as spiritually mature as they should be. It's because they haven't taken the next step: obedience to God's Word.

The Bible is a book unlike any other because it comes with a spiritual imperative to be obeyed. We are to read the Bible with the goal of obeying—putting into practice—what it says. It is that second step that begins to reveal maturity in the life of the believer. God instructs us through the Bible in the path of godliness; and as we obey those instructions, we find ourselves actually moving toward maturity.

We noticed, in the previous lesson, how the people of Israel immediately obeyed what they heard as Ezra read from the Book of the Law. Israel had ignored God's commands concerning the Feast of Tabernacles—so they immediately set about to correct that disobedient behavior. In this lesson, we will use their actions, described in Nehemiah 8:13-18, as the basis for our study of obedience to the Word of God.

Obedience is perhaps the best single word to sum up the heart of our relationship with Christ. God is our Father, and obeying Him is our duty as His children. But we are also stewards of God —His representatives, bearing His image on the earth. Obedience to the master is the primary responsibility of a steward in any setting. From more than one perspective, obedience is the heart of our relationship with God.

God revealed Himself to us through the Word for a reason; there are objectives He means to accomplish in the human race. And He means to use His spiritual children to accomplish those objectives. Therefore, it only makes sense that obedience to His revelation is our primary responsibility in the Christian life. The Bible is a book to be read in order to get our marching orders in fulfilling our calling by God into His grand purposes.

Through Israel's response to God's revelation we can make five observations about the nature of obedience.

OBEDIENCE IS RELATED TO HUNGER

It is plain that the "heads of the fathers' houses of all the people, with the priests and Levites" were hungry "to understand the words of the Law" (verse 13). They had already stood for several hours listening to Ezra read the Word the day before, and "on the second day" they returned to him for more!

J. N. Darby has written, "To be hungry is not enough. I must really be starving to know what is in God's heart toward me. When the prodigal son was hungry, he went to feed upon the husks; but when he was starving, he turned to his father." [1]

To "hunger and thirst for righteousness" (Matthew 5:6) means to be desperate; to fear dying unless one is fed. That's apparently how the people of Israel felt when they heard Ezra read from the Book of the Law. They had not been fed the Word of God for decades and decades. There had been a famine of the Word of God in their land (Amos 8:11). So for eight days, as they fulfilled the Feast of Tabernacles, they feasted on obedience to the Word (verse 18).

The spiritual giant, A. W. Tozer, wrote this about those in Church history who have a great legacy:

> I venture to suggest that the one vital quality which they had in common was spiritual receptivity. Something in them was open to heaven, something which urged them toward God. Without attempting anything like a profound analysis, I shall say simply that they had spiritual awareness and that they went on to cultivate it until it became the biggest thing in their lives. They differed from the average person in that when they felt the inward longing, they did something about it. As David neatly put it, "When thou saidst, 'Seek ye my face;' my heart said unto Thee, Thy face Lord, will I seek." [2]

What Tozer is identifying is the hunger for God seen in the lives of great men and women. These individuals wanted more than anything to obey God. And to know how to obey God, they had to be consumers of His Word. This doesn't seem complicated, yet there are few who hunger for God and His Word in that way. When we can echo those words of David in our lives, we will find ourselves in the company of those who have impacted the world for Christ—those who have manifested a hunger for God's will above all else.

OBEDIENCE IS RELATED TO HUMILITY

Of the group that approached Ezra—fathers, grandfathers, priests, Levites—some, if not many, were likely younger than Ezra. Certainly the priests and the Levites might have considered themselves superior in some way to him. Yet they humbled themselves and came to Ezra saying, "Teach us—we want to learn." Humility is a prerequisite for spiritual growth.

The Bible speaks often to the subject of humility and its opposite, pride. The book of Proverbs warns us not to be wise in our own eyes (3:7), that there is more hope for a fool than for such a man (26:12). Isaiah 5:21 says, "Woe to those who are wise in their own eyes, and prudent in their own sight," and Romans 12:16 expressly commands, "Do not be wise in your own opinion."

Those verses are in the Bible to remind us that the person who is full of himself has no room for God. A man who thinks he knows everything already is going to find scant reason to call upon God. A humble person is definitely one who knows that he does not know everything. In fact, compared to what he needs to know about God, he knows very little! We can choose to agree that we know little, or we can let God teach us—usually in a painful way. I definitely recommend choosing humility to begin with. God's "School of Humility" is a curriculum every believer takes until he learns the spiritual advantages of putting away pride.

Remember, the men and leaders who approached Ezra were graduates of a seventy-year-long "School of Humility" held in Babylon. They were not eager to repeat that course, so they humbled themselves before Ezra and asked him to teach them God's Word.

J. I. Packer, a man whose writings I greatly appreciate, once wrote, "Not till we have become humble and teachable, standing in awe of God's holiness and sovereignty . . . acknowledging our own littleness, distrusting our own thoughts and willing to have our minds turned upside down, can divine wisdom become ours. It is to be feared that many Christians spend all their lives in too unhumbled and conceited a frame of mind ever to gain wisdom from God at all." [3]

Much as Nicodemus did in John 3, anyone who desires to be taught by God must first empty himself and become a humble student before Him saying, "Teach me, Lord."

OBEDIENCE IS RELATED TO HONESTY

The third observation is the heart of this section on obedience: Honesty is a large part of being obedient to God. A bit of background is necessary to appreciate what is happening regarding the Feast of Tabernacles.

The men and leaders of Israel were listening to Ezra read the Book of the Law. When he got to the portion of Leviticus that is numbered today as chapter 23:33-43, they were shocked to discover that they had not been keeping the Feast of Tabernacles. In fact, we read in verse 17 that the Feast had not been kept for over a thousand years, since the days of Joshua. Not even during the glory days of David and Solomon was the Feast of Tabernacles observed.

If that discovery had been made today, some Bible scholars would excuse us from fulfilling the responsibility by saying it was a "cultural" thing—that God surely wouldn't intend for modern, sophisticated people to build small huts and dwell in them for seven days to celebrate a religious observance.

But the people who listened to Ezra replaced religious sophistication with the innocence of children. They said, "God wants us to build huts and live in them for a week. That's what we'll do. Let's begin immediately!" In spite of cultural or intellectual or practical objections they might have raised, they chose to obey God's Word.

There is an honesty required when it comes to obeying God— a level of integrity and transparency that reveals no ulterior motives. The only motive is to please God by obeying Him in whatever He says to do—just as a servant (steward) would obey a master without question. Yes, we have to be discerning when it comes to separating things in Scripture that applied, for instance, only to the Jews in the Old Testament. Christians don't celebrate the Jewish feasts for that reason. But we must be careful not to use Bible interpretation as a way to avoid being obedient to God. It would be easy to say about matters in the New Testament, "We haven't done that for two thousand years. Surely God doesn't expect us to do it now!"

I often think about old Noah in the early chapters of Genesis, how God commanded him to build an ark to escape the great flood that was coming—at a time when it had never rained on earth. He must have looked foolish to those to whom he tried to explain his project. They didn't know what rain was because no one had ever experienced it. Yet Noah took God purely at His word and did what He said to do.

Until we can say to God, "I will do whatever your Word says for me to do—no excuses," we have not yet been honest with God or ourselves.

OBEDIENCE IS RELATED TO HABIT

In the final verse in this section, we learn that Ezra continued to read "day by day, from the first day until the last day" of the Feast—for eight days (verse 18). They couldn't get enough of the Word. Day after day they listened as Ezra read through the first five books of the Bible.

This touches something unusual about the Bible. Spiritual hunger works just the opposite of how physical hunger works. Spiritual hunger grows the more we feed it, but physical hunger grows the more we neglect it. If you neglect to feed yourself, you get increasingly more hungry. However, in the spiritual realm if you neglect to feed yourself, your hunger goes away. But if you do feed yourself, you get even more hungry! In fact, it is fine to overeat in the spiritual realm—you can never take in too much. Exercise? Absolutely. We need to use all those spiritual calories we're consuming in ministry to others. But making a habit of feeding ourselves regularly will lead to increased hunger.

One of the great privileges of my life is to be able to attend the Founders Week events at the famous Moody Church in Chicago. This week-long series of meetings is held in the historic Moody Church with its wraparound balcony—four thousand people pack out the meetings during the day and the evening. It is a marvelous place to be fed from the Word of God. The speakers fill the pulpit, one hour at a time, one after another: three speakers in the morning, then two in the afternoon, then two or three more in the evening. It is a non-stop, weeklong feast, and the people continue to come back for more, hour after hour. Some people come to all the messages during the entire Founders Week, just like the people did in Jerusalem when Ezra read from the Word.

Beginning with the invention of the printing press around 1450, followed by the Protestant Reformation in 1517, the Bible suddenly became widespread in Europe and, eventually, in the new world of America. People who had never seen or touched a Bible, much less owned one, suddenly had access to Scripture. And the Word of God was devoured by those who were starving to know God's truth — just like the Jews in Jerusalem when Ezra read from the Book of the Law.

If you don't feel a hunger for God's Word, you need to make a habit of consuming it. The more you eat, the more you will want to eat. Soon you will not be able to get enough.

OBEDIENCE IS RELATED TO HAPPINESS

Finally, we observe that obedience is related to happiness: "And there was very great gladness" (verse 17). Happiness is a result, a by-product, of knowing and applying the Word of God.

It must have been a happy feeling for the people in Israel that day to know that they were doing something that had been neglected for a thousand years. And that's the feeling that comes with obedience—knowing we have done the right thing and that God is pleased with our actions. This happens in all areas of the Christian life. Perhaps you have struggled with witnessing or with tithing or another area of obedience. The joy that comes when you set your feelings aside and choose to obey the Lord is unlike any other. You know that the Lord honors obedience, that the seed of obedience you have sown will result in a harvest of righteousness. The greater the challenge to your will, the deeper the joy that comes from obeying God's will instead of your own.

A holy day became a holiday—a day of celebration and joy—as a result of the people's obedience to God. Because every day is a holy day for those who follow Christ, every day can likewise be a holiday resulting in a lifetime of joy and celebration when we chose to obey the Lord. There is no joy in the world like the joy that comes from obeying God. And when we daily reflect on the blessings of God—as the Israelites did during the weeklong Feast of Tabernacles—we are given new motivation daily for obeying Him.

So, five observations on how obedience relates to various aspects of the spiritual life in Christ: Obedience is born out of hunger for God and His Word; obedience is a matter of humility as we seek from God what we could never attain by ourselves; obedience is a matter of honesty before God's requirements; obedience feeds on obedience so that it becomes a lifestyle; and obedience is the truest source of happiness in the Christian's life.

Can you identify each of these five observations and connections in your own life? Step one toward renewal and maturity is to get into God's Word, and step two is to begin to obey it.

Notes

1. Quoted in Martyn Lloyd-Jones, *Studies in the Sermon on the Mount, Volume 1* (Grand Rapids: Eerdmans, 1959), 81.

2. A. W. Tozer, *The Pursuit of God* (United States: Christian Publishers, 1968).

3. J. I. Packer, *Knowing God* (Downers Grove: Intervarsity Press, 1973), 101.

1. Read Matthew 5:6.

    a. What kind of hunger did Jesus identify in this verse?

    b. What promise did He make to those who are hungry and thirsty for righteousness?

    c. What would characterize a person who hungers and thirsts for righteousness?

2. Read Nehemiah 8:13-18.

    a. How does verse 13 make it clear that the people were hungry for God's Word?

    b. For how long did the people listen to Ezra read "the Book of the Law of God"? (verse 18)

    c. In what way did the priests and Levites humble themselves?

d. Why is it important to choose humility, not pride, in your life?

e. What character trait that reveals no ulterior motives must Christians possess when it comes to keeping the Word of God? Explain how the Israelites demonstrated this character trait in verses 14-18.

f. What is a by-product of knowing and applying the Word of God? (verse 17) Describe a time when you have experienced this in your own life.

3. Why is it healthy to get into the habit of daily Bible reading?

a. How do you maintain the habit of reading God's Word each day?

b. What happens when you fall out of that habit? How can you prevent this from happening?

1. Discuss as a group how spiritual hunger works differently than physical hunger.

   a. If comfortable, share an example of a time when you were hungry for God's Word.

   b. What can we do to develop a greater hunger for God's Word?

2. Read the following verses as a group: Proverbs 3:7; 26:12; Isaiah 5:21; Romans 12:16.

   a. What do each of these verses teach us about humility and pride?

   b. Discuss the importance of humility in relation to spiritual growth.

3. Read Nehemiah 8:13-18 together.

   a. In what way was honesty a part of the Israelites' obedience to the Book of the Law that was read to them by Ezra?

   b. Share with the group how you have developed and maintained the habit of daily Bible reading in your life. How can you grow as a group in this daily habit?

c. For how many days did the people fulfill the Feast of Tabernacles? (verse 18)

d. When the Israelites finally completed the Feast, what emotion resulted? (verse 17)

e. Discuss how it makes you feel when you do the right thing and know that God is pleased with your actions.

4. Read Psalm 1:1-2 as a group.

a. What connection do we find between happiness, habits, and the Word of God in these verses?

b. How can you as a group encourage each other to "delight... in the law of the Lord" (verse 2) this week?

DID YOU KNOW?

A total of twelve feasts and sacred days filled the Jewish calendar in the Old Testament. (The last, Purim, was instituted near the end of the Old Testament period.) Of the twelve occasions, three were designated as most important by God: Passover, the Feast of Weeks (also known as Pentecost), and the Feast of Tabernacles (or Feast of Booths). For these three major feasts, all the Jewish males were required to appear before the Lord to celebrate— either at the tabernacle prior to the building of the temple, or at the temple in Jerusalem (Exodus 23:14-19). Passover, first on the calendar, was the most important of these three as it commemorated the Hebrew slaves' exodus from Egypt.

Step Number 3:

GETTING CONCERNED ABOUT SIN

Nehemiah 9:1-37

In this lesson we encounter one of the most beautiful prayers in the Bible — a prayer of brokenness before God.

OUTLINE

Every Christian sins, but not every Christian reflects on the fact that God is faithful even when we are a failure. That is the story of humanity throughout the Bible: God's faithfulness, man's failings. When Scripture revealed their sin, Israel was moved to confess and repent before God.

I. They Repented in a Spirit of Brokenness

II. They Reflected Upon Their Blessings

III. They Recognized Their Sinfulness

W e are following the experience of the returned remnant of Israelites to Jerusalem from their captivity in Babylon. They have rebuilt the wall around Jerusalem under Nehemiah's leadership and been convicted of their negligence to God's Word under Ezra's leadership. After completing a week of celebrating the Feast of Tabernacles for the first time in Israel in a thousand years, we now find them in a place of repentance (Nehemiah 9:1-37). Most of this long section of Scripture (verses 5-37) consists of a beautiful prayer recounting the grace of God in Israel's history.

This moment of repentance may have followed on the heels of the Day of Atonement, normally celebrated on the tenth day of the seventh month (Leviticus 16:29-30; Nehemiah 8:2). It is certainly in keeping with that occasion of reflecting on their sins. The people have moved from a period of celebration, beginning on the second day of the month (Nehemiah 8:13), to a time of deep introspection and penitent prayer.

This was not a casual moment. The people were "fasting, in sackcloth, and with dust on their heads. . . . and they stood and confessed their sins and the iniquities of their fathers" (verses 1-2). They read from the Book of the Law for "one-fourth of the day; and for another fourth they confessed and worshiped the Lord their God" (verse 3). This is a profound reflection of the conviction brought about by their intense exposure to the Word of God over the course of recent weeks.

Considered one of the most beautifully written compilations of prayers and services in the English language, the original Anglican *Book of Common Prayer* contains a confessional prayer known as "The General Confession." There are words spoken by the minister followed by the prayer of confession repeated by the congregation:

> The minister shall say: Dearly beloved brethren, the Scripture moveth us, in sundry places, to acknowledge and confess our manifold sins and wickedness; and that we should not dissemble nor cloak them before the face of Almighty God our heavenly Father; but confess them with an humble, lowly, penitent, and obedient heart; to the end that we may obtain forgiveness of the same, by his infinite goodness and mercy. And although we ought, at all times, humbly to acknowledge our sins before God; yet ought we chiefly so to do, when we assemble and meet together to

render thanks for the great benefits that we have received at his hands, to set forth his most worthy praise, to hear his most holy Word, and to ask those things which are requisite and necessary, as well for the body as the soul. Wherefore I pray and beseech you, as many as are here present, to accompany me with a pure heart, and humble voice, unto the throne of the heavenly grace, saying—

To be said by the whole Congregation, after the Minister, all kneeling: Almighty and most merciful Father; we have erred, and strayed from thy ways like lost sheep. We have followed too much the devices and desires of our own hearts. We have offended against thy holy laws. We have left undone those things which we ought to have done; and we have done those things which we ought not to have done; and there is no health in us. But thou, O Lord, have mercy upon us, miserable offenders. Spare thou those, O God, who confess their faults. Restore thou those who are penitent; according to thy promises declared unto mankind in Christ Jesus our Lord. And grant, O most merciful Father, for his sake; that we may hereafter live a godly righteous, and sober life, to the glory of the holy name. Amen.[1]

Surely that invitation to prayer, and prayer of confession, is in the same spirit that was present on the day of confession in Jerusalem in 445 B.C.

I encourage the study of this great prayer in Nehemiah 9 in detail. But for purposes of this lesson, we will identify three principles that reflect the spirit of biblical confession.

THEY REPENTED IN A SPIRIT OF BROKENNESS

I cannot recall many occasions on which I have witnessed today's Christian Church, the Body of Christ, praying and repenting as a group before God. I believe it was more prevalent in prior generations—especially during the periods of revival that swept various regions of America—but we have not witnessed corporate confession much in my memory. I have witnessed brokenness in individuals as they confessed their sins to God, but not often in groups.

True revival and renewal spring forth from ground that is watered by the tears of brokenness, confession, and repentance. Sadly, confession today seems to arise on the heels of being caught in sin. It becomes difficult to know whether people are sorry for their sin or sorry their sin was discovered. The people of Israel seem to have been expressing an historical sense of the nation's separation from God. They seemed to be genuinely convicted by their, and their fathers', participation in sin such as comingling with their godless neighbors (verse 2).

THEY REFLECTED UPON THEIR BLESSINGS

It seems odd that, in the midst of a lengthy confessional prayer, there would be so much space given to recounting the blessings of God. But there is—beginning in verse 6. Verses 6-8 cover the period from Creation to Abraham; verses 9-15 from the wilderness wanderings to entering the Promised Land; and verses 26-31 from the judges to the Babylonian captivity.

The point of these reflective verses can be summarized as the theme of this prayer: God's faithfulness and man's failure. Two phrases occur to illustrate that theme: "But Thou . . ." (God's faithfulness) and "But they . . ." (man's failure). We wonder how a nation as blessed as Israel could have sinned against God. But is that not what we ourselves do? It is the story of God's saving grace in every generation: We sin; God saves.

In verses 6-15 note the repetition of the connecting word "and." It serves to connect all the acts of God on behalf of the people of Israel: and, and, and, and. God's saving acts go on and on throughout Israel's history—and ours. Anyone who has walked with God for any length of time could (and should) recite the same kind of history of what God has done in his life. We would run out of paper and pen before we ran out of God's blessings in our life. On our worst days, when things look the darkest, such a recounting of God's faithfulness will give us the strength and faith to trust Him yet further in our lives. God's faithfulness makes our worst days better than the best days of those who don't know Christ.

In this prayer God is noted as the God of creation (verse 6), grace (verse 7), answered prayer (verse 9), deliverance (verses 10-12), revelation (verse 13), and supply (verse 15). He is described as merciful, great, mighty, just, and good. But man is described as proud, rebellious, disobedient, evil, sinful, and wicked. The prayer switches from God's faithfulness to man's sin, back to God, back to man, from verses 6-31. Every time man sinned, God was faithful to step in and rescue, forgive, reestablish—whatever Israel needed. But in spite of God's faithfulness, Israel would sin again. That is the history of God's dealing with His chosen people—and again, with us. When we sin, God is there to wrap His arms around us and restore us to Himself. And in spite of His forgiveness, we forget and sin again. God's faithfulness, man's failure—the theme of this prayer and of our lives as well.

We often talk of God as the "God of the second chance." But He is really the God of the third, fourth, tenth, and hundredth chance! However often we fall, He hears our cries of confession and restores us to a place of fellowship with Him.

An exercise worthy of our time and attention is to pause and reflect on our own cycle of "God's faithfulness, our failure." Anybody who does that seriously will be moved to pray a prayer of thanks to God just as the Israelites did that day; a prayer that mingles the record of His faithfulness in spite of our failures, time after time.

THEY RECOGNIZED THEIR SINFULNESS

The first principle is that the people repented in a spirit of brokenness. Then they reflected upon their blessings. And finally, we find them recognizing their sinfulness. As they confessed their *sins* to God, they saw their *sinfulness* all the more clearly.

Here is their confession (verses 32-33) which came after recounting God's faithfulness in spite of their failures:

Now therefore, our God,
The great, the mighty, and awesome God,
Who keeps covenant and mercy:
Do not let all the trouble seem small before You
That has come upon us,
Our kings and our princes,
Our priests and our prophets,
Our fathers and on all Your people,
From the days of the kings of Assyria until this day.
However You are just in all that has befallen us;
For You have dealt faithfully,
But we have done wickedly.

That is biblical confession. Biblical confession means something very specific: to say the same thing as God says. The Greek word for confess is *homologeo*, which is comprised of two words: *homo* (same as) and *lego* (to speak). When we confess our sin, we must say the same thing about our sin as God does. God speaks plainly and does not stutter, and neither should we. We call our actions mistakes, errors, tendencies, foolishness—anything but sin. Our fleshly nature does not like to admit that it is sinful. But if we are going to be honest in our confession before God, we must call our actions what God calls them: sin.

Confession means to say, "God, You are right, and I am wrong. What I did violates Your standards, and I shouldn't have done it. I am sorry for my sinful behavior. I agree with You that my actions were sinful. I confess my sins before You and ask for Your forgiveness." True brokenness comes when we see our actions and words the same way God sees them. We will not grieve over them until we view them from His perspective. Nor will we appreciate God's faithfulness fully until we have appreciated the darkness of our sin, which only comes from agreeing with God about it.

I want to give you a list of self-examination questions from the heart and pen of a famous revivalist and evangelist named Alan Redpath. He was an Englishman who conducted much of his ministry in the United States. I remember to this day when he died in 1989—I was participating in a Bible conference in Florida when word came of his death. The next day, the Moody radio network conducted a live conference call with men like Warren Wiersbe and Ian Leach participating, during which they recounted the spiritual depth and influence of Alan Redpath. He was particularly used by God to point out the necessity of living a life of holiness after being saved.

Consistent with that message was a section in one of his books in which he talked about an all-night prayer meeting he held—just he and God alone, together. He used a series of questions to probe his own heart, to discover the sins he needed to confess to God. Here is the first category:

What about my relationship with men?

- Am I consciously or unconsciously creating the impression that I am a better man than I really am?
- Is there the least suspicion of hypocrisy in my life?
- Am I honest in all my words and acts?
- Do I exaggerate?

- Am I reliable?
- Can I be trusted?
- Do I confidentially pass on what was told to me in confidence?
- Do I grumble and complain in the church?

Then he asked himself . . .

- Am I jealous?
- Am I impure?
- Am I irritable and touchy and distrustful?
- Am I self-conscious, self-pitying, and self-justifying?
- Am I proud?
- Do I thank God I am not as other people?
- Is there anyone I fear or dislike or criticize or resent? If so, what am I doing about it?

Then came . . . What about my devotion to God?

- Does the Bible live in me?
- Do I give it time to speak to me?
- Do I go to bed in time and do I get up in time?
- Am I enjoying my prayer life today?
- Did I enjoy it this morning?
- When I am involved in a problem in life, do I use my tongue or my knees to solve it?
- Am I disobeying God in anything or insisting upon doing something about which my conscience is very uneasy?
- When did I last speak to someone else with the object to try to win him to Christ?
- Am I a slave to books or dress or friends or work or convention?
- How do I spend my spare time?

Alan Redpath said those questions caused him to search his life at a level so deep it took him all night to get through the process. And I believe they would do the same for anyone who will take time to bring each question before God in the spirit of Psalm 139:23-24: "Search me, O God, and know my heart; try me, and know my anxieties; and see if there is any wicked way in me, and lead me in the way everlasting."

Sometimes we don't know what's in our own heart, but the Spirit of God does (John 2:24; Acts 1:24; 15:8). Therefore, if we take time to ask Him to search our heart and show us what we can't see, we will likely be able to confess (agree with God) more fully. That doesn't mean we should become spiritually, obsessively introspective, spending large blocks of time trying to discover long-buried roots of current problems in our life. But it does mean we should pray regularly that God would show us our own heart—and sometimes to use lists like Alan Redpath's to probe more deeply than we can on a daily basis. The world we live in is so fast-paced that unless we purposefully set aside time for such inquiry, it won't happen as often or thoroughly as needed.

On the wall in a YMCA building in Albany, New York, is a plaque with these words: "Prayer is like a golden river at whose brink some die of thirst while others kneel and drink." Such is the prayer that we find in Nehemiah 9. To some it will be a long, historical recounting of history. They will miss the significance of the interplay between God's faithfulness and man's failures. Others, however, will kneel and drink. They will be struck by the parallel of their own life to that of Israel.

This prayer is a waystation on the road to renewal. Don't pass by in such a hurry that you fail to be refreshed.

Note

1. *The Book of Common Prayer* (New York: The Church Pension Fund, n.d.), 5-6.

1. Read Nehemiah 9.

   a. Why did the Israelites separate themselves from the foreigners? (verse 2)

   b. For how long did the people read from the Book of the Law? (verse 3)

   c. How much time did they spend in confession and worship? (verse 3)

   d. In your own daily time with the Lord, how much time do you make for confession and worship? Why are those important daily habits to develop as a Christian?

e. In verse 6, what did the Levites begin to do?

f. What different periods of blessing did the Levites recount in verses 6-31?

g. List some different times where God has blessed you in your own life. Why is it important to recount God's blessings in the midst of confession?

2. Read 1 John 1:9.

   a. What promise is made to those who confess their sins?

b. Do you believe your relationship with God can be fully restored when you confess your sins to Him?

c. Explain what it means biblically to confess one's sins.

3. Read through the list of questions Alan Redpath used to examine his heart and discover sins he needed to confess to God. (See "They Recognized Their Sinfulness.")

   a. Which of these questions can you begin to ask yourself daily, weekly, or monthly?

   b. How do you think beginning the practice of examining your heart will help you become more Christlike?

GROUP QUESTIONS

1. Read Nehemiah 9:1-5 as a group.

   a. Describe how the Israelites were assembled according to verse 1.

   b. Why did the people devote time to confessing their sin and worshiping God?

2. Read Nehemiah 9:6-31 together.

   a. List some of the different ways God is described in these verses. (See verses 6, 9, 13, and 15 specifically.)

   b. Discuss the periods of blessing the Levites recounted in these verses.

c. Read Psalm 106. How is this passage in Nehemiah similar to Psalm 106?

d. What do both of these passages teach us about the importance of recounting God's blessings?

e. This prayer switches back and forth between man's sin and God's faithfulness. How do we see the cycle of "God's faithfulness, our failure" play out in our own lives?

3. Discuss what biblical confession means.

a. Why are we to call our actions sin like God calls them?

b. How does biblical confession lead to true brokenness and grief over our sin?

c. Read Psalm 139:23-24 and review the list of questions that Alan Redpath used to examine his own heart before God. If comfortable, share with the group which of the questions you want to begin asking yourself on a regular basis and why you chose those questions.

DID YOU KNOW?

Nehemiah 9:5-38 is the longest prayer recorded in the Bible. It is one of three long prayers in the Old Testament, all of which are easy to remember because of their similar chapter designations: Ezra 9 (verses 6-15), Daniel 9 (verses 4-19), and this prayer in Nehemiah. Like the recounting of Israelite history in Nehemiah, there are three other places in Scripture where such a recounting takes place: Psalm 78 (a psalm of Asaph, 72 verses long), Psalm 106 (by an unnamed psalmist, 48 verses long), and Acts 7 (Stephen's defense before the Sanhedrin in Jerusalem, 53 verses long).

Step Number 4:

GETTING CAUGHT UP IN WORSHIP

Nehemiah 9:1-37

*In this lesson we examine the process
and practice of biblical worship.*

OUTLINE

No one can claim to have discovered the exact elements of a New Testament worship service. It's not in the Bible. What the Bible does give us are principles of process and practice that should be reflected in our worship. The form of biblical worship may vary, but the focus cannot.

I. The Process of Worship
   A. Worship Is the Result of Concentrating on the Scriptures
   B. Worship Is the Response of the Confession of Our Sin
   C. Worship Is the Reverence for the Majesty of God
   D. Worship Is the Reaction to the Works of God

II. The Practice of Worship
   A. It Is Not Just an Experience, It Is an Expression
   B. It Is Not Passive and Melancholy, It Is Powerful and Majestic
   C. It Is Not About Someone, It Is to Someone

Most modern people like instruction books: Do this, connect that, then do steps 1–3. And in some cases the Bible gives us clear directives in areas of the spiritual life. But worship is not one of those areas. There is no place in the New Testament that says, "In order to worship Jesus Christ you must . . . ." Instead, we have examples of people worshiping at various places throughout Scripture, and from them we draw principles that we apply to our own worship experience.

But just because we are not given "five steps" to effective worship doesn't mean it is not important. Worship of our Creator-God is "man's chief and highest end" (Question 1, *The Westminster Larger Catechism*).

I am told that a lady once asked Albert Einstein to send her a short definition of his theory of relativity. He wrote to her saying, "If you sit on a park bench with your best girl for two hours, it seems like two minutes. If you sit on a hot stove for two minutes, it seems like two hours." That is relativity, according to Einstein. If we apply Einstein's definition to church services, it might go like this: If you attend a ball game for two hours, it seems like two minutes. But if you attend church for two minutes, it seems like two hours. The theory of spiritual relativity!

I wonder if the reason worship services seem like "two hours" is because the average Christian is a spectator instead of a participant. We are going to find principles in Nehemiah 9 that will inform our understanding of what it means to participate in worship. The Israelites spent a fourth of the daylight hours—a good three or four hours—confessing to and worshiping the Lord their God. And that was following another three or four hours spent listening to the Word of God. Christians today would likely recoil at the thought of spending that much time in Bible study and worship on the same day.

THE PROCESS OF WORSHIP

There are four principles having to do with the process of worship.

Worship Is the Result of Concentrating on the Scriptures

Verse 3 is clear about the order of events: They read the Word of God for a fourth of the day followed by worship. The latter was certainly motivated by the former. That was the connection also in the other two lengthy, worshiping prayers I mentioned in the previous lesson: Ezra 9 and Daniel 9. In both cases worship followed an encounter with the Word.

Have we organized our worship services backward? As I have already stated, there is no rule about this in Scripture. But typically in modern churches, we worship first and then hear a message from Scripture. This might be an area to consider revising based on the principle of worship flowing from interaction with the Word.

Worship Is the Response of the Confession of Our Sin

Twice (verses 2 and 3) we are told that the Israelites confessed their sins corporately before God. There is a euphemism employed in the Old Testament of "lifting up holy hands," that is, hands unstained with blood. When the Israelites came to worship God, they were to have "no blood on their hands"—that is, no unconfessed sin.

Jesus echoed that idea by teaching that, if we are on our way to worship and remember that our brother has something against us, we are to go and settle things with our brother before proceeding with worship (Matthew 5:23-26). And in Matthew 18:15-17 Jesus reverses the field, saying if we have something against our brother because of his sin against us, we are to go immediately to him and be reconciled.

In either case, the goal is not to have outstanding spiritual debts when we come to worship, but to confess our sins and come with clean hands and a clean heart. Perhaps worship has become less meaningful to many because of a willingness to tolerate sin, to live with a defiled conscience. We haven't cleansed ourselves before coming into God's presence.

An excellent model for confession is found in verse 33: "For you have dealt faithfully, but we have done wickedly." As noted in a previous lesson, confession is saying the same thing God says which is not easy to do: God is just, and we are unjust. Worship springs from an appreciation that we have sinned but God has forgiven us. But if we don't confess that we have sinned, it takes away our motivation to worship God for His forgiveness.

Worship Is the Reverence for the Majesty of God

Verses 5-7 reveal the perception of God's majesty held by the Levites: He is "exalted above all," the Lord alone, the Maker of heaven "with all their host, the earth and everything on it, the seas and all that is in them," the Preserver of all creation, and the "Lord God." Clearly, the reading of the Book of the Law of Moses had refreshed the Israelites' memory on why God is deserving of worship. And it will do the same for us.

Worship is getting caught up in the nature and attributes of God—caught up in who God is. If you read through the confessional prayer in Nehemiah 9 and underline all the references to the character of God—His acts and being—you will create a mini-course for yourself in "Theology Proper," which is the category of systematic theology that deals with the attributes and existence of God. And you will have more than enough reasons to worship Him.

I want to quote an extended portion from a book by Jack Hayford, who describes his own experience with the majesty of God. He and his wife were traveling throughout the British Isles:

> We stood in silent awe sensing God's presence as shafts of sunlight arrowed through the gracefully arched windows high on the vaulted towers of the vacant abbey. The British countryside was welcoming another summer's morn as we ambled through the partially restored ruins of this ancient house of worship. Although for the most part it was disheveled and dilapidated. A dignity remained, which was only a trace of the beauty it had known six centuries before at its dedication.
>
> That summer as we had traveled, the whole nation was enjoying a certain regal festivity as the silver anniversary of Elizabeth's coronation as queen was being anticipated. It was amid this prevailing era of rejoicing in royalty that we were introduced to England. Millions of common folks of ordinary means were enthused and excited about

celebrating one woman's royal ascent a quarter of a century earlier.

This was not a case of idolatry or an instance of the mindless masses cowering before a royal tyrant with no choice of doing otherwise. On the contrary, the people were rejoicing. The entire kingdom possessed a general mood of personal and national significance, and it seems inescapably linked in some mystical way to the fact that each one perceived himself linked with and personally represented by the one who wears the crown and bears the scepter.

To a visitor from another country there seems to be a national dignity that flows to the general citizens from the regal office of a single individual who reigns over them exercising authority as a noble friend rather than a feudal overlord.

Then a second thought exploded. This is the essence of the relationship Jesus wants us to have with his church. He wants the fullness of his power, the richness of his nature, the authority of his office, and the wealth of his resources to enable our identity and determine our destiny.

Notwithstanding deep emotion filling my soul, a holy calm, and genuine joy possessed me. Standing there my gaze sweeping over the scene once again, verdant lush fields, fragrance of roses everywhere, magnificence and architecture with a stateliness of historic bearing I gently squeezed my wife's hand and I said "majesty." The word was crisp in my mind. "Majesty," I thought. "It's the quality of Christ's royalty and kingdom glory that not only displays His excellence, but which lifts us by His sheer grace and power, allowing us to identify and share in His wonder. Majesty."

As Queen Elizabeth's throne somehow dignifies every Englishman and makes multitudes of others partakers in a commonwealth of royal heritage, our ascended Savior sits enthroned and offers His regal resources to each and every one of us. "Majesty."

As Anna and I drove down the narrow highway, the road undulating from one breathtaking view to another, I said to her, "Take the notebook and write down some words." I began to dictate the key, the musical notes, the time value of each, and the lyrics. And I wrote this song:

Majesty, worship His majesty.
    Unto Jesus be all glory, honor and praise!
    Majesty, kingdom authority.
    Flows from His throne, unto His own, His anthem raise.
    So exalt, lift up on high the name of Jesus.
    Magnify, come glorify Christ Jesus the King.
    Majesty, worship His majesty.
    Jesus who died, now glorified, King of all kings.[1]

When you come to grips with the majesty of God, it changes your life. As the presence of the Queen of England gives dignity to every one of her subjects, the presence of the Lord on His throne in glory gives to each one of us a sense of identity.

Worship Is the Reaction to the Works of God

Nehemiah 9:17 contains a statement that should arrest anyone who claims to be a loyal subject of God: "And they were not mindful of Your wonders that You did among them," speaking of the Israelites of old. Could that be written of many of us, that we are not mindful of the mighty works God has done in our midst? God is a God who works among us continually (Mark 16:20). The question is, Do we recognize and remember the works He has done?

The prayer in Nehemiah 9 is filled with action words that describe what God had done in creation and among the Israelites. But before we criticize them for not being "mindful" of God's "wonders," we must ask ourselves if we are any more mindful than they were. When God does something in our lives, we need to build a monument in our heart—and in a diary, journal, or photo album—to provide a reminder for the future of His faithfulness. The Israelites were often commanded to build monuments for the sake of future generations, and we should do the same.

THE PRACTICE OF WORSHIP

Now we come to that aspect of worship about which I have already stated that Scripture gives no specific guidelines—the kind of guidelines that would answer the question, How do we carry out a New Testament worship service? While I can't prescribe an "order of worship" for churches, I can provide three principles that I believe are biblical and which should be reflected in every worship experience.

It Is Not Just an Experience, It Is an Expression

We often hear people talk about the experience of worship. The word *experience* suggests something that is happening for me or to me. We hear people say they attend a certain church because they love the worship—they love how it makes *them* feel.

There is nothing wrong with enjoying or feeling moved by worship, but that is certainly not the primary focus of biblical worship. The focus of biblical worship is on God, not on us. The purpose of biblical worship is to express our love to God, not to meet our expectations. Whatever good things happen to us during worship is a by-product of the love we express to God.

When we worship God, we are not just saying, "Praise Jesus, praise Jesus, praise Jesus" over and over. For what are we praising Him? Worship is centered on the content of His character. There are so many reasons to praise God! We need to engage our minds and direct our praise to Him for the good things He has done. As we continue to praise Him that way, we will never forget them. We will always be "mindful of [His] wonders" (verse 17).

It Is Not Passive and Melancholy, It Is Powerful and Majestic

If you review the setting of the great prayer of Nehemiah 9, you will find energy and activity, not passivity. The people were standing and confessing their sins (verse 2); the Levites "cried out with a loud voice to the Lord their God" (verse 4), then called on the people to "Stand up and bless the Lord your God forever and ever!" (verse 5) This was not a sleep-inducing worship service filled with people nodding in the pews. This was a loud, passionate, energetic service in which people were engaged in worship.

True worship will call all our senses to alert. For instance, if you were in a worship service (or any kind of meeting), and Secret Service agents walked in followed by the President of the United States, what would you do? When the president is announced, as a sign of respect and honor for the office, everyone stands to their feet.

If Jesus Christ walked into our worship service, in person, we would probably stand and then fall to our knees. Should we have any less of an attitude of engagement when the Lord Jesus Christ is present by His Spirit? Yes, there are moments of quiet reflection during worship. But even that is active engagement—not a moment for mind-wandering.

The more majestic our view of God, the more majestic will be our worship of Him.

It Is Not About Someone, It Is to Someone

Worship is a matter of the correct preposition: It's not *about* Someone, it's *to* Someone. The second person singular pronoun "You" occurs in the ninth chapter of Nehemiah more than forty times, all but one being a reference to God. Does that sound like worship that is general or specific? That is worship directed toward God. When you enter into worship, do you have God himself in mind as you sing and pray? Is your worship directed toward Him specifically?

Think about how odd it would be for me to express appreciation to my wife, directly to her, in the third person: "I love Donna, and Donna is wonderful. Donna just does a wonderful job in our family. Isn't Donna wonderful? She keeps a beautiful home, and it is so wonderful to be married to Donna. I just love Donna." Donna would be listening to this thinking, "What is David's problem?"

Donna wants to hear how I appreciate her, but she wants me to express it to her directly: "Donna, I love and appreciate *you*. *You* make such a world of difference in my life and in our family." Do you think God feels the same way?

Regardless of the specific order of the aspects of our worship, if we make it a powerful expression of our love for God, directed to God, it will be biblical worship.

Notes

1. Jack W. Hayford, *Worship His Majesty* (Waco: Word Books, 1987).
2. John Ayto, *Dictionary of Word Origins* (New York: Arcade Publishing, 1990), 577.

1. Read Nehemiah 9:1-37.

   a. What did the Israelites' worship and praise follow? (verse 3)

   b. What did the people do before they listened to the Word and worshiped the Lord? (verse 2)

   c. Why do you think it is necessary to confess our sins before entering worship? (See Matthew 5:23-26.)

   d. In what way is worship the response of your confession of sin?

   e. What do verses 5-7 reveal about how the Israelites viewed God?

   f. What did the Israelites learn from the past that helped them grow in their walk with God in the future? (verse 17)

g. Did the Israelites talk about God in their worship or to God?

h. While you worship, are you able to recognize God's great works like the Israelites did? If not, what can you do differently in your worship?

i. List a few of the reasons you have for praising God in your life right now.

2. What aspects of your own worship of God are most consistent with the points and principles made in this lesson? Which are in need of maturing?

   a. Most consistent:

   b. In need of maturing:

3. What aspects of worship today do you find that parallel what you have read in Nehemiah 9?

1. Discuss what you think might happen if Christians gathered and spent several hours confessing and worshiping the Lord followed by three to four hours listening to the Word of God on the same day.

2. Read Matthew 5:23-26 and 18:15-17 as a group.

   a. What do these verses teach us about the importance of confessing our sin before going to worship God?

   b. How does coming to worship with unconfessed sin hinder our worship of God?

   c. How does confessing our sin before worship impact our worship?

   d. Explain how Nehemiah 9:33 is an excellent model for confession.

3. Read Nehemiah 9:5-7 together.

   a. What words or phrases reveal the perception the Israelites had of God's majesty?

b. How does understanding God's majesty change our view of confession and worship?

4. Read Nehemiah 9:17 as a group.

   a. How is the phrase "And they were not mindful of Your wonders that You did among them" a reminder for us today?

   b. Are we mindful of what God has done for us? Why or why not?

   c. Share with the group a specific way you have seen God work in your life in the last year. When everyone is finished sharing, spend time in prayer, praising God for all He has done in each of your lives.

5. Based on the points and principles found in this lesson, discuss why it is justified to invest time, talent, and treasure in preparation for worship services on Sunday.

DID YOU KNOW?

Our modern English word *worship* has its origins in Old English (the twelfth century). It is derived from the original combination of *worth* and *ship*—a suffix that indicated state or condition. *Worthship* originally was used to denote distinction, credit, or dignity, but soon evolved into a word for respect and reverence. It began being used in religious contexts in the thirteenth century.[2] When we worship God, we are certainly declaring His "worth" or "worthiness: "You are worthy, O Lord, to receive glory and honor and power; for You created all things" (Revelation 4:11).

Step Number 5:

BECOMING ACCOUNTABLE FOR CONDUCT

Nehemiah 9:38-10:31

In this lesson we discover what it means to make a commitment to uniqueness.

OUTLINE

God created a race called the Jews. They were to be a "peculiar" people—distinct from all others in their character and conduct. Nehemiah called the remnant from Babylon to reaffirm their commitment to "peculiarity" by renewing their obedience and accountability to God's covenant.

I. The People Who Signed the Covenant

II. The Promises They Made in the Covenant
   A. They Vowed to Separate Themselves From the World
   B. They Vowed to Be Subject to the Word of God
   C. They Vowed to Set Apart the Sabbath

III. Conclusion

OVERVIEW

Depending on your age, you may be familiar with the original Volkswagen Beetle, the little German auto that was wildly popular several decades ago. It changed very little on the outside year after year while improvements continued on the inside. They got great gas mileage and ran "forever." Eventually, they went off the market and then returned in an updated style and sold well. The Volkswagen Beetle had what marketing experts call a Differential Advantage—something that set it apart from all the other cars on the road. It was the most unique car of its era.

Regardless of how old you are, you likely know little about the Ford Edsel—one of the biggest failures in auto design history. It lasted only three years: from 1958–1960. It had been wildly promoted as an experimental car and audiences were eager to see the new auto Ford had promised. But when it appeared, car buyers were overwhelmingly disappointed. It turned out to be an amalgam of shapes and parts of existing Ford products. In short, it lacked a Differential Advantage and was removed from the market due to poor sales.

We can take the idea of a Differential Advantage—a uniqueness or peculiarity—and apply it to God's chosen people, the Jews. The Jews have what no other race of people on earth has ever had: a covenant with Almighty God. In the Old Testament, when Israel followed God's covenant, they were successful in everything they did. They were looked upon as odd by the surrounding nations, but that was part of their strength. It was their relationship with God that made them different and gave them their advantage.

After coming into the Promised Land, the people decided they didn't like being a peculiar people; they wanted to be like their neighbors. They demanded of Samuel the prophet that he should pick a king for them like the other nations had. Samuel tried to warn them about replacing God with a human king to rule over them, but they wouldn't listen. So they were given a king, Saul, who turned out to be a disadvantage instead of an advantage. Throughout the Old Testament, whenever the Jews diluted their distinctiveness by becoming more like their neighbors, they lost more of their blessing.

After living in Babylon for seventy years and returning to Jerusalem to rebuild their city and temple, the Jews had a lot of work to do to regain their distinctive, covenant relationship with God: their Differential Advantage. The second half of the book of Nehemiah is about Israel's quest to recover her uniqueness as God's chosen nation. In this lesson we look at the fifth of ten steps Israel took to renew her spiritual commitment and maturity: becoming accountable for conduct.

In Nehemiah 9:38, we find the Jews making a "sure covenant," signed and sealed by the leaders, Levites, and priests. They made themselves publicly accountable for keeping God's standards, a return to being God's unique people by keeping His covenant requirements.

THE PEOPLE WHO SIGNED THE COVENANT

First in the list of those agreeing to the covenant is Nehemiah, followed by 83 others: 22 priests, 17 Levites, and 44 others who are called "leaders." More important than all the names that are given are two things stated in chapter 10, verse 28: They were people who had "separated themselves from the peoples of the lands [and joined themselves] to the Law of God" and who had "knowledge and understanding." In other words, they were making a conscious, informed decision about turning from the world back to their God. This wasn't an emotional meeting based on crowd dynamics. Every person who signed the covenant did so with "knowledge and understanding." They were making themselves accountable to God and to one another.

It was not only the men who are named who were involved. Their "wives, their sons, and their daughters" (verse 28) joined in the commitment as well. So it was everyone from Nehemiah to the priests and Levites, to the leaders and their wives and children who committed themselves to become accountable for their conduct before God.

THE PROMISES THEY MADE IN THE COVENANT

The covenant stipulations to which they committed themselves can be examined under three headings: separation from the world, subjection to the Word of God, and setting apart the Sabbath.

They Vowed to Separate Themselves From the World

They vowed to "walk in God's Law, which was given by Moses the servant of God, and to observe and do all the commandments of the Lord our Lord, and His ordinances and His statutes" (verse 29). That commitment was to have an immediate expression: not intermarrying with their pagan neighbors (verse 30).

From the earliest days of the Hebrew nation, intermarriage had taken a toll on the descendants of Abraham. It was not just intermarrying that was the problem—it was the ultimate spiritual syncretism that resulted in idolatry and immorality. Leaving the true God's commands led to worshiping the false gods of those they married. Idolatry was almost always the end result of intermarriage.

This is not just an Old Testament problem, not just a prohibition for the Jews. It is very difficult for a New Testament Christian to marry someone who does not love Christ and expect to continue to mature in the faith. It is for that reason that the New Testament is explicit about the dangers of being "unequally yoked" (2 Corinthians 6:14-18). Christians today should make the same covenant commitment that the Jews made in Nehemiah's day, that they will not marry those who are not believers in Christ.

That significantly limits a Christian's options for a marriage partner. But it does so in the same way that limitations in all of life result in keeping us safe. Marriages are the result of a first date. If Christian young people will never allow themselves to get emotionally involved with someone they don't consider a possible marriage partner, they will save themselves great grief and heartache later.

I counsel young people in our church to look down the road and think about the kind of marriage and family they want to have—then plan their dating life accordingly. It would even help to put it in writing, just as the people in Nehemiah's day did—write it in the front of your Bible or another permanent place: "I commit to dating and marrying a person who is committed to Jesus Christ. I will not compromise my testimony or my faith in this area. I vow to remain separate from the world in this most sacred area of my life." And then sign and date it; perhaps have a good friend sign it as a witness to your commitment.

Making that commitment won't guarantee a life of marital bliss. But it will increase the possibilities.

They Vowed to Be Subject to the Word of God

Not only did they vow to separate themselves from the world in their marriages, they vowed to be subject to God's Word (verses 28-29).

Here is the important thing to note: They weren't just committing themselves to become better students of God's Word (important as that is). They were committing to "walk in," "observe," and "do all the commandments of the Lord our Lord" (verse 29). The purpose of Bible study is not just to know the Bible, but to *do* the Bible— to put into practice what God has stipulated for us to walk in. The two aspects of commitment to God's words are never expressed more concisely than in Joshua 1:7-8 where the phrase "observe to do" is used twice. First, we "observe" (learn, study) and then we "do." We learn the Bible in order to do the Bible. In modern Bible study terminology, we would call those steps interpretation (observing) and application (doing).

The Bible really comes alive when we treat it as a book to fulfill rather than just a book to know; a book where we find our marching orders for the day instead of a historical record of what other people did. When we develop the learn-obey, learn-obey cycle in our daily routine, the Bible takes on a whole new life. And our lives take on a whole new level of maturity. Surprisingly, to many people, the more we obey God's Word, the greater our understanding becomes, the "sharper" our eyes become when we study. The more we do, the more God reveals to us.

They Vowed to Set Apart the Sabbath

This third commitment of the Jews doesn't apply directly to the Christian Church since we don't celebrate the Sabbath. The Sabbath was a Jewish ordinance that, along with the rest of the Jewish law, is not carried forth in direct application to the Church. (The Early Church began to meet for worship on the day of Christ's resurrection, the day following the Sabbath, the day we now call Sunday.)

But in Nehemiah's day, the Sabbath was the rule of God for His people. Part of the covenant they made was to reinstitute the laws governing the Sabbath so as to honor that day as God intended (verse 31).

After the wall around Jerusalem was rebuilt, a thriving commercial district developed outside the city walls. Vendors from the surrounding area would set up shop and cater to the people of Jerusalem on the Sabbath (verse 31). The Jews weren't working on the Sabbath, but they were treating it like a commercial day for buying and selling, which violated the purpose of the Sabbath as a day of rest.

The Christian Church has complicated this issue of the Sabbath by applying a lot of the Old Testament regulations to the day we call Sunday. They've turned Sunday into the New Testament Sabbath —which is not biblical. The only one of the Ten Commandments that is not repeated as a New Testament requirement for holy living is number four, to keep holy the Sabbath day.

Here's how I differentiate between the Old Testament Sabbath and the New Testament Sunday: The Sabbath was to be kept H-O-L-Y, and we are to keep Sunday W-H-O-L-L-Y for the Lord. Setting aside one out of seven days for rest is a creation ordinance, not a Jewish law. Therefore, while we are not under the obligation to keep the laws of the Jewish Sabbath, we ought to recognize the value of setting aside one-seventh of our life as a way to honor the way God created us, to give that day over wholly to the Lord to refresh ourselves—mentally, spiritually, and physically. It's a wonderful way to honor Him and His creation plan for human beings. It's a way to say to people who don't have a similar pattern in their lives that we live this way to honor the God of the Bible and His Son, Jesus Christ.

The people also renewed their commitment to support the Lord's work (the ministration of the temple and its services) (verses 32-34). We will look more closely at this step in their spiritual renewal in the next lesson.

CONCLUSION

What kind of Differential Advantage do we enjoy as Christian believers? Do people recognize us as being different from the world?

Let me conclude with this bit of verse written by John Fischer. I believe he makes the point as well as it can be made:

> "In it, not of it" the statement was made
>   When Christian One faced the world, much afraid.
>   "In it, not of it" the call was made clear,
>   But Christian One got something stuck in his ear.
>   "Not in it, or of it" was the thing that he heard.

And knowing the world was painfully absurd,
He welcomed the safety of pious retreat,
And went to the potluck for something to eat.

Now Christian Two, he knew what to do,
He'd show those fundies a thing or two!
How will the world ever give Christ a try
If we don't get in there and identify?
So "In it, and of it," he said in his car,
As he pulled in and stopped at a popular bar.
"I'll tell them the truth as soon as I'm able
To get myself out from under this table."

Along comes Christian Three jogging for Jesus,
In witnessing sweats made of four matching pieces.
His earphones are playing a hot Christian tune
About how the Lord is coming back soon.
"Not in it, but of it" he turns down the hill
And stops in for a bite at the Agape Grill.
Like the gold on the chain of his "God Loves You" bracelet,
He can have the world without having to face it.

Way up in heaven they lament these conditions
That come from changing a few prepositions.
"Not in it, or of it" Christian One thought.
But who in the world will know that he's not?
"In it, and of it," thought Christian Two.
But who in the world will know that he knew?
"Not in it, but of it" thought Christian Three.
But who in the world watches Christian TV?

And the Lord said to Gabriel, shaking His head,
"In it, not of it. Wasn't that what I said?" [1]

If we would keep our prepositions straight, we would end up
maintaining our Differential Advantage. God has not called us to
leave the world. But He has called us to live in it in a particular
way—to be a testimony to Him and our relationship with Him. We
are to be "in" the world but not "of" the world. We would
maintain no advantage for God whatsoever if we were to depart
this world or sequester ourselves away behind blinds and curtains.
The world needs to see God, and He has ordained that it see Him
in us. We are to be neither isolated from the world not imitators of
the world. We are to live in the world in such a way that our
uniqueness stands out.

Over time, we are to be "Beetles," not "Edsels"—something new and different that stands the test of time, not a religious remake of a bygone era. May God grant us grace to protect our Differential Advantage in Christ.

Note

1. John Fischer, *Real Christians Don't Dance* (Minneapolis: Bethany House Publishers, 1988), 132.

1. Read Nehemiah 9:38.

    a. How did the Israelites make themselves accountable in keeping God's standards?

    b. Who sealed the covenant?

2. Read Nehemiah 10:28-34.

    a. What did the leaders make a conscious decision to do in order to fully follow the Lord?

    b. Describe a time in your life when you separated yourself from negative influences so that you could turn toward the Lord.

    c. What did all the Israelites commit to do in verse 29?

    d. Explain why it is important not just to read the Bible but also to obey it.

    e. In verses 30-31, what commandments did the Israelites vow to keep?

f. Based on your knowledge of the Old Testament, what happened when the people intermarried with those who were not Jewish?

g. What did the people commit to support? (verses 32-34)

3. Read 2 Corinthians 6:14-18.

a. What contrasts did Paul use to explain the importance of being separate from the world?

b. Why is it important for believers not to be "unequally yoked" with unbelievers?

4. What does it mean to be in the world but not of it?

a. In contrast, what does it not mean?

b. In what ways can this phrase be misunderstood or applied incorrectly?

GROUP QUESTIONS

1. Discuss the concept of a "Differential Advantage" mentioned at the beginning of the lesson.

   a. How does this concept relate to the Israelites?

   b. How does this concept relate to New Testament Christians?

2. Review the "Did You Know?" section of the lesson.

   a. What were the two types of covenants made in the Old Testament?

   b. Explain how God's covenant with Israel through Moses was a conditional covenant.

3. Read Nehemiah 10:28-34 as a group.

   a. According to verses 29-31, what did all the people commit to do?

   b. Why was it important for them to separate themselves from the pagan nations around them? What had happened to them in the past when they had disobeyed this command?

   c. How were the Israelites currently treating the Sabbath?

d. While we do not need to keep the Sabbath as New Testament Christians, why should we wholly set aside Sunday for the Lord?

4. Read 2 Corinthians 6:14-18 together.

   a. What is the overall theme of this passage?

   b. How is this a follow-up to the pattern established in the Old Testament? (See Deuteronomy 7:3.)

   c. How do Paul's questions in verses 14-15 cast this issue as one of logic?

   d. How does verse 15 take an Old Testament principle and apply it to the New Testament?

DID YOU KNOW?

Covenants were common among the peoples of the ancient Near East. While covenants could be made between peers, such as the covenant between Abraham and Abimelech (Genesis 21:27), they were more common (and official) when binding a greater party (king) to a lesser party (subjects). In such a case, the covenants could be unconditional (the promise of unconditional blessing or protection) or conditional (promises made on the basis of compliance with obligations). God made unconditional covenants with Noah (Genesis 9:1), Abraham (Genesis 15), and David (2 Samuel 7). God's covenant with Israel through Moses was conditional (Exodus 19–24; Deuteronomy 28).

Step Number 6:

TAKING A PLEDGE TO GIVE

Nehemiah 10:32-39

In this lesson we learn what it takes
to put God first in giving.

OUTLINE

It has been said that a person's checkbook will reveal what is most important in that person's life. Jesus said that one's heart and treasure can be found in the same place. The Jews who returned from Babylon to Jerusalem made a commitment to put God first with their resources.

   I. **A Priority**

  II. **A Plan**

 III. **A Proportion**

 IV. **A Purpose**

  V. **A Place**

 VI. **Conclusion**

Throughout history, spiritual renewals and revivals have always touched the subject of financial stewardship. Why? Because our attitude toward money is usually the clearest measure of our attitude toward God. It was Jesus who said, "For where your treasure is, there your heart will be also" (Matthew 6:21).

Look in a person's checkbook and you will get a clear idea of where his heart is. If there is little or no money being directed toward God or those in need, then it calls into question what he says about his love for God or others. Spending most of our money —especially our discretionary funds, on ourselves, may indicate that we treasure ourselves more than anything else. I don't believe it is possible to be walking in complete fellowship with God and not have our money reflect that. We can't serve two masters (Matthew 6:24).

When the Jews in Jerusalem, under the leadership of Ezra and Nehemiah, recommitted themselves to walk in covenant with God, they committed their material possessions as well. They were operating under the Old Testament law and so they had specific responsibilities to fulfill with regard to their money. Although we don't live under the law today, there are still many principles of the law that can inform our spiritual practices today. And that is certainly true with regard to being good stewards of our finances.

A PRIORITY

Reading through Nehemiah 10:35-37, you find the terms "first-fruits" and "firstborn" used several times. The word "first" is used intentionally—the Israelites gave the first portion of everything to the Lord. Rather than doing something else with the first of the harvest (pay debts, spend it on themselves), God was the priority; God got the first of everything. And the same should be true of us today: God should be the priority when it comes to how we use what He has given to us.

Christians in modern economies become so burdened with debt and monthly financial obligations that God gets shuffled to the bottom of the stack. But when God ceases to be a priority, the burdens become even greater. To neglect God with material possessions is to cut off the hand that feeds us. Whether in the Old Testament or the New, God must be the priority among His people. He must get the first of everything: time, talent, and treasure. The pressure is always there to ask God to wait to become less of a priority. But when there is a commitment to put Him first, the negotiations end. That's the commitment the Israelites included in their renewed covenant with God.

A PLAN

Notice the time markers in verses 32-35: "yearly," "at the appointed times year by year," "year by year." The Israelites' agricultural economy worked on an annual cycle, and they made plans to gear their giving accordingly. In other words, they had a plan by which they expressed their material commitment to God. Too many Christians today don't have a plan—they give on an emotional or funds-available basis. And their blessings are just as sporadic and undependable as their giving.

First Corinthians 16:1-2 contains instructions from the apostle Paul to the church at Corinth to set aside their monies for the Jerusalem relief fund "on the first day of the week" so they weren't scrambling for money to donate when Paul arrived. The first day of the week, of course, was our Sunday—the day the church met together. So the plan was to give each Sunday in anticipation of Paul's visit.

We give by grace, not by law, in the New Testament era. But that does not mean sporadically or haphazardly. While the instruction to give "on the first day of the week" was tied directly to the Jerusalem relief fund, the principle of planned, systematic giving is thoroughly biblical. Whether the cycle was based on the harvest or preparation for a one-time relief gift, making God the priority means that we give to Him just as consistently as He gives to us.

In 2 Corinthians 9:7 we are told to give as we *purpose* in our heart—*purpose* meaning "to choose beforehand." Again, our giving is to be considered and intentional, not impulsive and occasional. We should develop a plan for our giving—an annual plan is probably a good idea for the average person—and then stick to it.

The average church goes through significant peaks and valleys with their income. There are occasionally good reasons for that, like farm-based seasonal incomes, downturns in the economy, and others. But the biggest reason is the unplanned, sporadic giving of church members. That would not have been the case with the renewed covenant signed by the Israelites in Jerusalem. They committed themselves to a plan for giving.

A PROPORTION

There are proportions mentioned in the Israelites' plan for giving: "one-third of a shekel" in verse 32 for the temple tax; ten percent (the tithe) in verse 38 for the Levites; one percent ("a tenth of the tithes") in verse 38 for temple services. This was not hit-or-miss giving. They knew exactly how much to give and when.

A tithe is ten percent, and there were three tithes in the Old Testament. First was the temple tithe, supporting the Levites in their ministry in the temple. Then there was the festival tithe to support the annual feasts of the Jews. Then there was a benevolence tithe that was collected every third year (equaling 3.33 percent annually). So the total giving for the Israelites was 23.33 percent of their income annually.

There were also other forms of giving in the forms of sacrificial offerings, the one-third of a shekel temple tax (verse 32), lost income from the land during the Sabbath rest year, lost repayment of loans every seven years when debtors were forgiven, and so on. So the Israelites knew exactly what their material obligations to the Lord were.

If Israelites were required by law to give ten percent of their income, how much more should we who live under grace give? Too many Christians plan their giving on the basis of how little they think they have to give in order to "get by" rather than how much they can give as an expression of gratitude to God for His rich blessings.

Here is an interesting perspective from St. Augustine, one of the esteemed fathers of the Church: "Our forefathers abounded in plenty because they gave God tithes, but now because our devotion toward God has receded, the imposition of taxes has advanced. We were unwilling to share with God, giving Him the tenth, and now the whole is taken from us. The tax gatherer takes from us that which Christ was not able to gather." One wonders how the prosperity of our own nation might change if Christians made tithing to God a priority in their lives.

A PURPOSE

The purpose for all this planned giving was for the Israelites to conform themselves to what was "written in the Law" (verse 34)—the law they had neglected for generations. The Jews had just returned from seventy years of exile in Babylon for neglecting God's statutes, an exile that had been predicted by Moses (Deuteronomy 28:36). Their motivation for obeying God's law was high! So they purposed to make their commitment to God and His law to avoid a similar circumstance again. They also gave as not to "neglect the house of our God" (verse 39). God's law, God's temple—God was their renewed purpose in life.

A PLACE

Another phrase that runs throughout this passage—eight times—is "house of our God," referring to the temple in Jerusalem. God has always had a place throughout redemption history to which the people of God brought their sacrifices, gifts, and offerings. The temple was the place in the Old Testament, and the local church is the place in the New Testament. God's people were to meet together and offer to God their gifts and offerings in a central place.

Some believe that all giving should be done to one's local church, but I prefer the principle found in Galatians 6:10, what I call priority giving: "Therefore, as we have opportunity, let us do good to all, especially to those who are of the household of faith." The household of faith—the local church—is where our spiritual needs are met and that is where the priority of our giving should be. The local church can only carry out its ministry as God's people give faithfully to it. But that doesn't mean every penny of your giving must go through the local church. In my own radio and television ministries, we are careful to encourage people to give first to their local church before giving to Turning Point Ministries.

Committed believers will be involved faithfully in a local fellowship of believers and will make it the priority in their material giving.

CONCLUSION

Dr. J. Vernon McGee, the venerable pastor and radio preacher, now with the Lord, told this story in his commentary on Nehemiah 10:32-39:

> I remember when we attempted to remodel the church in downtown Los Angeles, California where I served as pastor. The church in its long history had never been remodeled and the seats, which numbered four thousand, were built to take care of people who lived fifty or sixty years ago, and we discovered that people today are about two and a half inches wider than they were fifty years ago. So, we decided to put in new cushioned seats.

> Some of the very pious folks said, "We don't feel that money should be spent for cushions; we should give that money to missions." Now the majority of the people wanted the cushioned seats and I did, too, so I made a proposition to the congregation. I said "There are so many people enthusiastic about remodeling that they are going to give enough money to cushion their seat and yours, too,

so those of you who don't want to pay for cushioned seats can give your twenty-five dollars to missions, and I hope that we can take an offering today for several thousand twenty-five dollar checks."

Well, there were very few twenty-five dollar checks because the truth was that the folk who were objecting to the cushioned seats never intended to give at all, and missions instead of cushions, was their excuse. But what they said was, "It isn't God's will to have cushioned seats. The time hasn't come to remodel the church."[1]

I thought when I read that, "Things don't change much. Dr. McGee fought the same battles fifty years ago that are fought in the Church today." When peoples' money is involved, they can suddenly change their mind about what they believe is, or isn't, God's will.

One of the prophets who ministered in Israel during the time of Ezra and Nehemiah was Haggai—a prophet who is unfamiliar to many in the Church today. His message was to the Jews at a time when they had lost the vision and motivation for completing the work of rebuilding the walls of the city and the temple. It will serve us well to consider a lengthy passage from Haggai, chapter 1:3-15:

Then the word of the Lord came by Haggai the prophet, saying, "Is it time for you yourselves to dwell in your paneled houses, and this temple to lie in ruins?" Now therefore, thus says the Lord of hosts: "Consider your ways! You have sown much, and bring in little; you eat, but do not have enough; you drink, but you are not filled with drink; you clothe yourselves, but no one is warm; and he who earns wages, earns wages to put into a bag with holes." Thus says the Lord of hosts: "Consider your ways! Go up to the mountains and bring wood and build the temple, that I may take pleasure in it and be glorified," says the Lord. "You looked for much, but indeed it came to little; and when you brought it home, I blew it away. Why?" says the Lord of hosts. "Because of My house that is in ruins, while every one of you runs to his own house. Therefore the heavens above you withhold the dew, and the earth withholds its fruit. For I called for a drought on the land and the mountains, on the grain and the new wine and the oil, on whatever the ground brings forth, on men and livestock, and on all the labor of your hands."

Then Zerubbabel the son of Shealtiel, and Joshua the son of Jehozadak, the high priest, with all the remnant of the people, obeyed the voice of the Lord their God, and the words of Haggai the prophet, as the Lord their God had sent him; and the people feared the presence of the Lord. Then Haggai, the Lord's messenger, spoke the Lord's message to the people, saying, "I am with you, says the Lord." So the Lord stirred up the spirit of Zerubbabel the son of Shealtiel, governor of Judah, and the spirit of Joshua the son of Jehozadak, the high priest, and the spirit of all the remnant of the people; and they came and worked on the house of the Lord of hosts, their God, on the twenty-fourth day of the sixth month, in the second year of King Darius.

The Jews were taking care of their own needs first instead of God's. They had provided houses for themselves before providing a "house" (temple) for God. They were keeping everything for themselves for fear of running out. They had forgotten the promises of Deuteronomy 28 that if they walked in God's commandments, they would never run out of anything that they needed.

I have seen over the years that people who put God first by tithing of their income live better on the ninety percent that is left than they did on the one hundred percent they used to keep for themselves. Giving to God is like having children: If you wait until you think you can afford it, you'll never do it. But when we put God first financially out of obedience to Scripture, we find that God blesses that obedience, and we have what we need.

We never know what our faithfulness to God with our finances might accomplish. I read of a young soldier during World War II who faithfully sent a tithe of his wages home to his mother in America, asking her to give it to the church fund for a new Sunday school building for the young boys in his class. When he returned from the war, he found a beautiful building had been built and named in his honor. The congregation had been so convicted by his faithfulness in putting God first that they began to do the same, and funds for the new building were quickly gathered.

Our faithfulness in putting God first might be what He uses to spark a renewal in the lives of others.

Note

1. J. Vernon McGee, *Thru the Bible, Vol. 2: Joshua–Psalms* (Nashville: Thomas Nelson Publishers, 1983).

PERSONAL QUESTIONS

1. Read Matthew 6:21, 24.

   a. How did Jesus connect our finances to our relationship with Him in verse 21?

   b. Is it possible to serve two masters according to verse 24? Why or why not?

2. Explain why God must be the priority in every area of your life, including your finances.

3. Read Nehemiah 10:32-39.

   a. What key term is found in verse 35 that relates to the Israelites' giving?

   b. What term is used in verse 36?

   c. Why do you think it is necessary to give the first of what God has given us back to Him?

d. What proportions are mentioned in the Israelites' plan for giving in Nehemiah 10:32, 38?

e. What reason did the Israelites have for tithing? (verses 34, 39)

4. What are some of the reasons you have for tithing?

   a. Do you tithe to your local church or other Christian organizations? Which are we called to tithe to first? (See Galatians 6:10.)

   b. Why is it important to tithe to your local church?

5. Read Haggai 1:3-15.

   a. What was the prophet Haggai's message to the Jewish people?

   b. What promise of God had they forgotten? (See Deuteronomy 28.)

   c. In what ways do Christians today put themselves first and God last when it comes to their finances?

1. Read Nehemiah 10:32-37 as a group.

   a. What words and phrases indicate that giving to God was to be their priority?

   b. Describe the plan the Israelites had for their giving.

2. Read 1 Corinthians 16:1-2 and 2 Corinthians 9:7 together.

   a. On what day of the week did Paul order the church to tithe? (1 Corinthians 16:1-2)

   b. How are we to decide when to tithe according to 2 Corinthians 9:7?

   c. Should our giving be considered and intentional or impulsive and occasional?

   d. Discuss some of the reasons we are supposed to tithe to our local church first.

e. What are some excuses Christians make for not tithing regularly or not tithing to their local church first? What can we do to combat the temptation not to tithe regularly?

3. Read Nehemiah 10:32, 38 together.

   a. What was the Israelites' plan for tithing?

   b. In what ways is having a plan for tithing helpful?

4. Read Haggai 1:3-15 as a group.

   a. Discuss the main point Haggai wanted the Jewish people to understand.

   b. Why is it tempting to take care of our own needs before tithing to our local church?

   c. If comfortable, share with the group a time when you saw God provide for your needs when you put Him first in your finances.

DID YOU KNOW?

The third-shekel offering (Nehemiah 10:32) probably has its roots in the half-shekel offering legislated in Exodus 30:13-14. Every man twenty years of age and older was responsible to pay this tax. This was also likely the tax that was collected by King Joash for the repair of the temple (2 Chronicles 24:4-14). The Jewish historian Josephus notes that Jewish men in the first century paid the half-shekel temple tax as mentioned in Matthew 17:24. The third-shekel tax in Nehemiah's day (instead of a half-shekel) may have been due to economic hardship. (Summarized from *The NIV Study Bible* notes on Nehemiah 10:32.)

Step Number 7:

OFFERING YOURSELF FOR SERVICE

Nehemiah 11:1-36

In this lesson we learn that every follower of Christ has an important job to fulfill.

OUTLINE

A standard joke in every work setting, whether business, church, or ministry, is that whoever is missing from a meeting gets "volunteered" for the worst jobs. But in God's economy, there are no worst jobs—only important ones. Saying, "Here am I! Send me," is precious in God's sight.

I. The Process Involved in Repopulating Jerusalem
   A. They Instituted a Draft
   B. They Asked for Volunteers

II. The People Involved in Repopulating Jerusalem
   A. The Groups
   B. The Words for the Groups

III. Concluding Principles
   A. Necessity, not Notoriety, Is the Rule of the Body
   B. Performance, not Preeminence, Is the Basis of Reward
   C. It's a Privilege to Be Drafted; It's Even More Precious to Volunteer

OVERVIEW

The essence of the Christian life is summarized by Paul in 2 Corinthians 5:7: "For we walk by faith, not by sight." Even in the "down times," when it seems there is no evidence of God at work in our midst, our responsibility is to continue to walk by faith, to live out of obedience to what we know God wants us to do.

There are seasons of abundance and seasons of dryness in the Christian life, seasons in the work God has called us to do. In some seasons there is more evident blessing than in others, but in all seasons the work goes on.

There must have been many in the Jewish community in Nehemiah's day who wondered whether God had forgotten them. The city of Jerusalem seemed to lie dormant with no evidence of God's blessing. The walls of Jerusalem had lain in heaps of rubble for 160 years before they were rebuilt by Nehemiah. Before Nehemiah rebuilt the wall, the temple was rebuilt by Zerubbabel. Prior to the work of these men, it might have appeared that God had abandoned Mt. Zion and His sacred city.

God gave Nehemiah a vision for rebuilding the walls around Jerusalem. He did an amazing job of organizing, delegating, and managing a very difficult task so that the wall was rebuilt in just over seven weeks. But once the temple and the wall were in place, we have discovered that there was another kind of building that remained: spiritual building—renewing the hearts and minds of God's people. And God used Ezra and Nehemiah to challenge the people to renew their commitment to God and His covenant stipulations.

Nehemiah 7-11 is a parenthetical part of the book where some of the problems associated with spiritual renewal were dealt with. One of the problems was that, even though the temple and the wall had been rebuilt, no one wanted to live in Jerusalem to defend it. There was apparently much fear among the people that Jerusalem might come under attack again and those living in the city be killed—as happened previously at the hands of the Babylonians.

So Nehemiah appointed two men—his brother, Hanani, and Hananiah—to be in charge of fortifying the city and building up the population within its walls (Nehemiah 7:1-3). The challenge was not small. The threat of enemies who might attack Jerusalem was so ever-present that Nehemiah instructed the two men not to open the city gates until noon.

So that was the setting for the story we pick up in Nehemiah 11:1—the repopulating of the city of Jerusalem.

THE PROCESS INVOLVED IN REPOPULATING JERUSALEM

Towns in Israel were small during this period—perhaps less than a dozen acres in size. Jerusalem was larger, of course, but built very compactly on the top of a mountain ridge for purposes of defense. Though the city was basically uninhabited for 160 years, it was time now for Jerusalem to regain its stature as the capital of Israel, the nation.

Chapter 11 opens with the leaders of the people casting lots to select ten percent of the population to become residents of Jerusalem, the other ninety percent remaining in their towns, scattered throughout the land.

They Instituted a Draft

The problem they faced then was not unlike the problems faced by many cities today: Everybody wants to live in the country. But the rebuilt city of Jerusalem needed inhabitants in order to build it up again as the major city in Israel. So they first instituted a draft—or the casting of "lots" (verse 1)—to select "one out of ten to dwell in Jerusalem" (verse 1). Note the connection of "lots" with our modern term "lottery." The Israelites believed God made His will known through casting lots (Acts 1:12-26; see "Did You Know" at the end of this lesson).

So ten percent of the population of Jews was "drafted" to inhabit the newly-walled city of Jerusalem.

They Asked for Volunteers

In addition to those chosen, the leaders also asked for volunteers: "And the people blessed all the men who willingly offered themselves to dwell at Jerusalem" (verse 2).

The Hebrew word for volunteer means to "willingly offer" as it is translated in verse 2. Something inside this group compelled them to say, "We need to set our own desires aside and make a contribution to the reestablishment of God's city and God's house." Jerusalem had been the epicenter of life in Israel for several centuries, and there were apparently many who caught that vision and volunteered to move in.

While preachers often dread the long lists of names that occur in various places in the Bible, their importance needs not to be overlooked. The lists of names from the descendants of Benjamin and Judah (the two tribes exiled to Babylon), from the priests, Levites, and gatekeepers point to the value of individuals. These were real people, with real hopes and dreams, who were part of a significant move in time and space to reestablish the city of God, Jerusalem. God knows the name of every person and family, especially the ones who volunteered, who moved back into the city. God also knows those today who serve Him—and we should recognize them as well.

THE PEOPLE INVOLVED IN REPOPULATING JERUSALEM

Not only are the names of individuals and families mentioned, but descriptions are given of the various groups that moved into Jerusalem. The groups then make me think of the various groups it takes to conduct ministry in any church today, and how important each is to the success of the ministry.

The Groups

There are five groups, five categories, of individuals mentioned in this chapter. The first group is made up of the draftees and volunteers whom we have already discussed.

The second group was those who did the work in the temple: 822 priests and other servants who carried out the continual ministrations of sacrifice and worship in the temple (verses 10-12).

The third group (verses 15-16) took care of affairs outside the temple: civil affairs, public service, running the city—remember that civil and religious affairs were all under the same heading. There was no separation of church and state, and no king. Nehemiah was creating a government to get the city going after everything was demolished by the Babylonians.

Fourth was Mattaniah, "the leader who began the thanksgiving with prayer" (verse 17).

The final group is mentioned in verse 22: Uzzi was "the overseer of the Levites at Jerusalem."

The Words for the Groups

Here are the descriptive terms I have applied to each of the five groups—terms that I believe will apply to those who seek to serve the Lord today.

- Occupation: These were the ones who moved back to occupy the city of Jerusalem, to be a godly presence in that place.
- Dedication: These were dedicated to doing the work in the temple. They were focused on that one area of life in Jerusalem. None of us can do everything, but all of us can do something with dedication and energy.
- Delegation: These had "oversight of the business outside of the house of God" (verse 16). They were city managers, if you will, responsible for a broad range of services within the city walls of Jerusalem.
- Consecration: Prayer and thanksgiving were in this group's job description. They led the people in "the sacrifice of praise" (Hebrews 13:15), the top priority of all who would worship God.
- Celebration: The Levites were in charge of Israel's spiritual life; they were the pastors of the people, leading them into truth, worship, and celebration.

We can apply those five descriptive terms to ministry in the body of Christ today.

Occupiers are the faithful members of the Body who vote with their feet, showing up whenever and however there is work to be done. *Dedicated ones* take their giftedness and calling from God seriously. *Delegators* are those with the gift of administration and leadership who can organize things and people to accomplish God's goals. *Consecrated ones* spend time interceding for the work of God so that it is accomplished in a spiritual, not a fleshly, manner. And *celebrators*—those who inspire the Body to lift up praise and worship to God.

Do you see where you fit in that list? Those are obviously not the only five categories of people we could name, neither then nor now. But the idea is clear: Every Christian fits in the Body of Christ somewhere. God hasn't saved anyone to do nothing. You might be an occupier, a dedicated worker, a delegator, a worship leader, or an intercessor—or you may have another calling from God altogether.

But whatever each believer has been gifted and called to do, the goal is the same: the unity of God's people to accomplish God's work, whether in Jerusalem or in your local church. We've noted the diversity of names, families, jobs, and roles in Jerusalem. So unity doesn't mean "all the same." Unity means a hand being different from a foot being different from an eye—yet all coordinating their work together for the unity of the body.

J. B. Phillips' translation of 1 Corinthians 12:29-30 says it well:

As we look at the body of Christ do we find all are his messengers, all are preachers, or all teachers? Do we find all wielders of spiritual power, all able to heal, all able to speak with tongues, or all able to interpret the tongues? No, we find God's distribution of gifts is on the same principles of harmony that he has shown in the human body.

The challenge for every believer in Christ is to discern what his role in the Body of Christ is, to learn what gift(s) God has given to him. And most of all, to understand that there are no "lesser" gifts in the Body. Every gift is important. (Given by God, how could it not be?) The Body of Christ can no more be complete without every member doing his part than the human body could be. Not to do your part is to deny others the service you are intended to render and to deny yourself the blessing of serving.

Just as God tore down the walls of Jericho without man's help, He could have rebuilt the walls of Jerusalem the same way. And He could carry out every aspect of His plan today without us—except the part of His plan where we are matured into the image of Christ by serving! God has chosen to use each individual who belongs to Him to accomplish certain things and to mature that individual in the process.

When God presents us with an opportunity—like the opportunity willingly to move back into Jerusalem—we should grasp it and embrace it. If we don't, the likelihood is great that we will look back one day and regret the missed opportunity to serve. Consider this parable as an illustration of what we're talking about in this lesson:

The Carpenter's tools had a conference. Brother Hammer was in the chair. The meeting had informed him that he must leave because he was too noisy. But he said, "If I am to leave this Carpenter's shop, Brother Gimlet must go too. He is so insignificant that he makes very little impression on anyone."

Little Brother Gimlet arose and said "Alright, but Brother Screw must go also. You have to turn him around and around again to get him to go anywhere."

Brother Screw then said, "If you wish, I will go, but Brother Plane must leave also. All his work is on the surface. There is no depth to it at all."

To this Brother Plane replied, "Well, Brother Rule will also have to withdraw if I do, for he is always measuring people as though he were the only one who is right."

Brother Rule then complained against Brother Sandpaper and said, "I just don't care. He's rougher than he ought to be, and he's always rubbing people the wrong way."

In the midst of these discussions, the Carpenter of Nazareth walked in. He came to perform his day's work. He put on His apron, and He went to the bench to make a pulpit from which to preach the Gospel to the poor. He employed the screw, the gimlet, the sandpaper, the saw, the hammer, the plane, and all of the other tools. After the day's work was over and the pulpit was finished, Brother Saw arose and said, "Brethren, I perceive that all of us are laborers together with God."

And so we are. We are the family of God whom God has called to serve in unity and in diversity.

CONCLUDING PRINCIPLES

Whether in Jerusalem or your local church, here are three principles that reflect eternal truth when accomplishing God's work.

Necessity, not Notoriety, Is the Rule of the Body

It matters not whether we are famous or exalted for what we do when serving Christ. It only matters that we are necessary. We were saved "for good works . . . that we should walk in them" (Ephesians 2:10). You are not necessary because you are famous; you are necessary because you are important to the unity of the Body.

Performance, not Preeminence, Is the Basis of Reward

Many of the names that appear in Nehemiah 11 are not found elsewhere in Scripture. Most of the people mentioned were not famous on earth. But they were famous to God. He knew their names not because they were preeminent in Israel but because they were faithful and willing to do a job for Him. And He will remember and reward followers of Christ for the same reason.

Hebrews 6:10 is a key verse in this regard: "For God is not unjust to forget your work and labor of love which you have shown toward His name, in that you have ministered to the saints, and do minister." God does not forget the work we do regardless of how menial it may seem to us.

It's a Privilege to Be Drafted; It's Even More Precious to Volunteer

Finally, being chosen and submitting to that choice is good. But being like the prophet Isaiah who said, "Here am I! Send me," reflects the heart of God (Isaiah 6:8). The ones in Jerusalem who "won the lottery" were blessed. It was a privilege to be able to move back into the city of God on earth. But there were others who said, "Here am I! Send me." Those volunteers who see a need in the Body of Christ and raise their hand without being asked reflect a measure of discernment and grace that is precious in God's sight.

If you are part of the work of God in your local church, God has something for you to do. If He calls and you say, "Yes," blessed are you. Even better, look around and anticipate the needs that are coming and say, "Here am I! Send me."

1. Read Nehemiah 11:1-36.

   a. What does it mean to cast lots? (verse 1)

   b. How many people were selected to become residents of Jerusalem?

   c. Where did the remaining population reside?

   d. For what reason do you think some willingly volunteered to live in Jerusalem? (verse 2)

   e. Did God recognize those who volunteered in that day, even though they were not well-known people?

   f. How many people did the work of the temple? (verses 10-12)

g. How many took care of the affairs outside the temple? (verses 15-17)

h. What do the lists of names found in this passage point to?

2. Do you think God recognizes when you volunteer for His work today? Why or why not? (See Hebrews 6:10.)

3. When was the last time you were "drafted" to serve in some nonprofit setting (neighborhood, church, or other)? What was your response?

a. When was the last time you saw a need and volunteered to meet it without being "drafted"?

b. How does Galatians 6:7 apply to the issue of volunteering for service in anticipation of a time when you might be in need?

4. Describe how each Christian is a necessary member of the Body of Christ. (See 1 Corinthians 12:29-30; Ephesians 2:10.)

1. Read Nehemiah 11:1-36 as a group.

   a. Why did the Israelites need to repopulate Jerusalem?

   b. How did the leaders go about deciding who would repopulate the city?

   c. Share about a time when you were "drafted" into a ministry and ending up growing in your Christian life as a result.

   d. List and describe the five groups mentioned in this chapter.

   -
   -
   -
   -
   -

   e. Discuss the five descriptive terms mentioned for the five groups.

   f. How do these terms relate to the Body of Christ?

   g. Does one of these terms apply to you? If so, share with the group which one and how you came to that conclusion.

   h. Why is it necessary for believers to discern where they belong on that list?

2. Read 1 Corinthians 12:29-30 together.

   a. Why is each member of the Body of Christ important?

   b. What are the results when we do not do our part within the Body of Christ?

   c. Discuss the importance and blessing of volunteering to serve within your local church.

3. Read Hebrews 6:10 as a group.

   a. What does this verse teach us about our work for God?

   b. How can this verse encourage you as you serve in your local church?

DID YOU KNOW?

Casting lots was a common practice among ancient cultures. It was practiced by the Persians (Esther 3:7), the pagan sailors on whose ship Jonah was running from God (Jonah 1:7), and the Roman soldiers vying for Christ's clothes at the crucifixion. It is also mentioned in other settings (Joel 3:3; Nahum 3:10; Obadiah 11). The Jews in the Old Testament used lots to determine the scapegoat (Leviticus 16:8), assign the tribes to their inheritance in the Promised Land (Joshua 18:10), discover a guilty person (Joshua 7:14), select a king (1 Samuel 10:20-21), and assign priests to their divisions (1 Chronicles 24:3-19). Lots were probably made of pieces of stone or bone with markings on them, analogous to modern dice.

Step Number 8:

GIVING THANKS FOR GOD'S GOODNESS

Nehemiah 12:1-47

*In this lesson we learn how thanksgiving
results in thankful living.*

OUTLINE

There should be a positive correlation between what we say we are
thankful for and the expressions of those thanks in practical ways.
When the Jews joyfully celebrated the dedication of the wall around
Jerusalem, their joy overflowed into expressions that were plain
to see.

  I. **Purification**

  II. **Procession**

  III. **Proclamation**

  IV. **Provision**

OVERVIEW

This series of lessons is all about spiritual renewal that leads to spiritual maturity. I have called them steps and taken them from the experience of Nehemiah and the process of rebuilding the city of Jerusalem—its temple and its walls. The seven steps we have studied so far are:

1. Getting back to God's Word
2. Getting serious about obedience
3. Getting concerned about sin
4. Getting caught up in worship
5. Becoming accountable for conduct
6. Taking a pledge to give
7. Offering yourself for service

In this lesson we look at the eighth step to renewal: giving thanks for God's goodness. The Scripture for our study is the twelfth chapter of Nehemiah.

Nehemiah's main task in Jerusalem was to rebuild the wall around the city, which he did: "So the wall was finished on the twenty-fifth day of Elul, in fifty-two days" (Nehemiah 6:15). But then the wall seems to disappear from the book. It is mentioned in 7:1, but not again until 12:27 when the wall was dedicated. What happened?

The wall disappeared from view from chapters 7–11 so that the other aspects of "rebuilding" could be highlighted: the spiritual rebuilding that was necessary for a people who had been out of touch with God for a long time. Rebuilding the wall around the city wasn't enough by itself. After all, the original wall had not been enough to deter the Babylonians who took the Jews into captivity. The people needed the spiritual protection that comes with walking in obedience to God.

So chapters 7–11 detail the spiritual revival that took place under the leadership of Ezra. He ministered the Word of God to the people so they could see what they had been missing. The wall was completed (6:15) and dedicated (12:27). But in between, the Jews were preparing themselves to live within that wall as a renewed people—and the dedication of the new wall was next on the agenda.

There are two Hebrew words that can be used for the idea of "dedication" (verse 27). One is a word that means "to consecrate" or "to set apart for God." That is not the word that is used here. The Hebrew word used in verse 27 means "to mark the beginning of a new thing." The dedication of the wall was more than just the completion of a project; it was the beginning of a new era in Israel's history and the history of Jerusalem.

We can identify four things that happened as a result of the dedication of the wall around Jerusalem.

PURIFICATION

The Levites had been summoned from all over the land for the dedication (verse 27). Once there, "the priests and Levites purified themselves, and purified the people, the gates, and the wall" (verse 30). That was a symbolic cleansing that spoke to God's desire for His people to be pure—even the gates and the wall! God wants everything with which He is associated to be pure.

Anyone who professes to be a follower of Jesus soon realizes that it is impossible to live like the world lives and remain pure in God's sight. The indwelling Holy Spirit came to convict the world of "sin, and of righteousness, and of judgment" (John 16:8). Therefore, every believer will be convicted of impure, unrighteous living, and will have a desire to be pure.

PROCESSION

The second part of the dedication was the appointment of two thanksgiving choirs led by the leaders of Judah, with Ezra following one choir and Nehemiah following the other (verses 31-39). One choir went in one direction around the top of the wall (it was wide enough for a procession of people to walk on) and the other in the opposite direction. The choirs were singing celebratory songs (psalms) giving thanks for what God had done.

We think in our modern era that we are the only ones smart enough to plan extravagant events like crusades, celebrations, festivals, and the like—that people in Nehemiah's day weren't sophisticated enough to do this. But this procession, indeed the entire dedication service, reflects a significant amount of planning and execution on the part of Nehemiah and others. They were intent on praising God and celebrating what He had done. They were putting forth their best effort to honor Him.

Everyone was represented—people, princes, and priests—because all had been involved in the project. It's a sad thing when God's people watch the 80/20 rule play itself out in the Body of Christ: where eighty percent of the work is done by twenty percent of the people. The eighty percent who didn't give much of themselves to the project find little to celebrate. The more we invest in God's work, the deeper our cause and capacity for celebration.

I remember attending the dedication service for a church's new facility in our community. I had friends in the congregation and knew the pastor well, but wasn't quite sure what to expect in the service since their worship style is a bit more "expressive" than ours. It all seemed very traditional until the pastor called on the people to express their thanks to God corporately for what He had done. And a cacophony of voices rose up in the church as people poured out their thanks to God for His blessings. I, along with most others in the room, had tears running down my cheeks as I witnessed an entire congregation emotionally involved in celebrating the work of God. They were excited and expressive because they had all participated in giving and building that new facility. I imagine that the voices of the choirs on the wall of Jerusalem that day were no louder than the voices of praise I heard in that new church building.

We had some friends in the Midwest who left a church over a minor disagreement right at the beginning of the building program. By the time the building program was finished, they had ironed out their differences and returned to the church. But they expressed to me how sad they were that they missed the joy and excitement of being part of the building program—of watching God work miracles and the church experience unprecedented unity.

If you want to be involved in the celebrations your church has —whatever the occasion might be—you need to invest yourself in the process. Otherwise, you will have little joy over what has been accomplished. Don't live on the defensive, looking for reasons not to be involved. God's plans are moving forward, and you should be part of them. Remember: The joy of the Easter resurrection was possible only because of the pain of Good Friday.

PROCLAMATION

The third thing that happened was proclamation: "Also that day they offered great sacrifices, and rejoiced, for God had made them rejoice with great joy; the women and the children also rejoiced, so that the joy of Jerusalem was heard afar off " (verse 43). I love the fact that it was their "joy" that was heard "afar off." What does joy sound like? Surely it involves singing, but not everyone has a great singing voice. Yet, even if you can't sing, you can still express joy in other ways: "Make a joyful shout to God, all the earth!" (Psalm 66:1) "Let us shout joyfully to Him" (Psalm 95:2). "Make a joyful shout to the Lord, all you lands!" (Psalm 100:1)

I know that their joy was not just over the completion of the wall but also over the rebuilding that had taken place in their own hearts and lives. All the steps we have seen so far led them to renewed commitments to walk in covenant with God, to obey His Word, to give, to be accountable for their conduct—and more. When God's people are walking in fellowship with Him, joy is the (super)natural spiritual result. Galatians 5:22 says that part of the fruit—the manifestation—of the Spirit's lordship in life is joy.

Somebody has said that joy is spelled J-O-Y, meaning that joy is Jesus and You with Zero in between. When there is nothing between you and Jesus, there is nothing that can diminish your joy. In other words, joy is the natural expression of a person who is connected spiritually and intimately with God. Joy will be there continually unless something comes between the two to short-circuit the experience—something called sin. Israel certainly had no joy in Babylon because their sins had come between them and their God. But now, they have been cleansed and made pure and renewed their commitment to Him—and their joy was heard "afar off."

Does anyone have more reason to be joyful than Christians? I think not. Charles Haddon Spurgeon, the great London preacher, was occasionally chided for his frequent use of humor in the pulpit. His reply was that if his listeners only knew how much he held back, they would commend him for his restraint instead of chiding him for his humor. The great reformer, Martin Luther, is said to have been a man who loved laughter, and who loved to have theology students in his home for meals that were characterized by wholesome fun as much as wholesome food.

There is no wonder the Jews' joy could be heard afar off. People who walk in the blessing of God have ample, ready reason to express joy at all times.

Proverbs 17:22 says, "A merry heart does good, like medicine." But Proverbs 15:13 says, "But by sorrow of the heart the spirit is broken." A broken heart and broken spirit go hand-in-hand, but a joyful heart lifts up the spirit. Remember: a joyful heart should be *normal* for those in right relation with God. If your spirit is downcast, look for what has gotten into your heart that is blocking your joy.

PROVISION

In verses 44-47, we find the last dynamic taking place as part of the dedication of the wall around Jerusalem: provision.

Once the people were settled into the city, surrounded by the newly-dedicated wall, basking in the glow of their covenant commitments and the joy that resulted, it was time to begin making practical applications based on their commitments. It was time to turn their thanks-giving into thanks-living. They wanted to begin thanking God with their hands as well as in their hearts.

Support for the Levites was the responsibility of all Israel. They had been given no inheritance of land in the Promised Land, but as the "worship leaders" of the nation, they were to be supported by tithes from the people. And as the people looked around, they realized that the Levites' stores needed to be replenished, that they needed to fulfill their responsibility to their spiritual leaders.

Even in the modern church, if every Christian were faithful to make God a financial priority in his life, there would never be a request made for more money. In fact, new churches could be started and a full-time pastor supported by just nine families committed to tithing. If nine families tithed their income to a church plant, there would be sufficient income to pay the salary of a pastor at an income level that averaged the same as the nine families. But because most Christians do not tithe of their income, churches usually are in a money-raising mode.

But in Jerusalem, the people took it upon themselves to meet their financial obligations to their spiritual leaders. This action flowed out of step number six, a commitment to give, discussed in lesson 6 of this study guide. Thanks-giving is always followed by thanks-living—learning to give in response to God's gifts to us.

I realize there are biblical, and nonbiblical, ways to encourage people to give. Assuming spiritual leaders are encouraging the saints in a biblical fashion, they will inevitably be met by resistance from some—those who say the pastor will kill the church (drive people away) by too much emphasis on giving. But the truth is, I've never heard of a church that died from giving too much! I've heard of some that dried up and went away because they never learned to give of themselves to serve others and extend God's

Kingdom. And I've heard of some that became more and more fruitful the more they gave. But I've never heard of one that died from giving too much. When believers give in a biblical fashion (humbly, generously, cheerfully, voluntarily), God seems to bless the church beyond measure. (I have also never had a Christian say to me, after more than four decades of pastoral ministry, "Pastor Jeremiah, I made a big mistake last year. I gave too much to God.")

That may sound facetious, but I'm being truthful about the need for Christians to learn what the Jews in Jerusalem learned—that we can trust God with our material needs and with our giving. As Paul expressed in Philippians 4 to those who had given generously to him, "And my God shall supply all your need according to His riches in glory by Christ Jesus" (verse 19). Stewardship is a matter of grace, not law. As God pours out His grace upon us and we respond by the power of that grace, His grace continues to flow and our needs are always met.

Consider these thoughtful, poetic words of Strickland Gilliland:

Steward I am, not possessor of the wealth entrusted me.
    What, were God Himself the holder, would His
        disposition be?
    Then I ask myself each morning, every noon and
        every night,
    As I view His gentle goodness with an ever new delight,
    Steward only, never owner, of the time that He has lent,
    How, were He my life's custodian, would my years on earth
        be spent?
    Thus I ask myself each hour as I plod my pilgrim way,
    Steeped in gratefulest amazement in His mercy day by day.
    Steward only, not possessor, of the part of Him that's I.
    Clearer grows this truth and dearer as the years go
        slipping by.
    May I softly go and humbly, head and heart in
        reverence bent,
    That I may not fear to show Him how my stewardship
        was spent.

Strickland has reminded us, in his old English style, that we are stewards and not possessors of what he have. His questions make us ask the same thing as the popular "What Would Jesus Do?" slogan: How would God use my money, my time, my possessions if they were His to spend? If God moved into your house today and had your money and time at His disposal, how would it be used? How would God live within our skin if He walked where we walk?

The people in Nehemiah's day answered those questions generously by fulfilling God's expectations of them. And we can do the same if we will take the same steps toward spiritual renewal that they took. When we take step one—a commitment to the Word of God—the rest of the steps fall in place, including this one.

1. Read Nehemiah 12:27-43.

   a. What did all the people, including the Levites, gather together for at the wall of Jerusalem? (verse 27)

   b. What was involved in this celebration? (verse 27)

   c. Once there, what did the priests and Levites do to themselves, the people, the gates, and the wall? (verse 30)

   d. What do you think the purpose of purification is? Why is purification important for you today?

e. In verses 31-39, what did the leaders do to show their appreciation to God for what He had done for them?

f. What message did the Israelites send to their neighbors by doing this?

g. According to verse 43, what proclamation did the people make at the wall?

h. How are we to make proclamations today? (See Psalm 66:1; 95:2; 100:1.)

i. How often do those around you "hear" your joy? Give some examples of how you "shout to the Lord" verbally or nonverbally.

j. List some of the reasons you have to be joyful as a Christian.

2. Read Nehemiah 12:44-47.

   a. How did the people support the Levites as part of the dedication of the wall around Jerusalem?

   b. Why was it the responsibility of the people to support the Levites?

1. Read Nehemiah 12:37-43 together.

   a. Explain the meaning of the Hebrew word used for "dedication" in verse 27.

   b. How did the dedication of the wall indicate a new beginning for Israel?

   c. Why was purification an important part of the dedication? (verse 30)

   d. Why should we desire to live pure lives today?

   e. Describe the procession found in verses 31-39.

   f. In what ways did this procession reflect the planning and preparation of Nehemiah and others?

g. Who was represented in this procession?

h. What is the value of processions? What do they say to the world?

i. How do Christians publicly proclaim God's blessings today?

j. If applicable, share with the group what kinds of processions you have been involved in for the sake of God's Kingdom.

2. Read Psalm 66:1; 95:2; 100:1 as a group.

   a. How do each of these verses describe praising the Lord?

   b. If comfortable, share with the group how you "shout to the Lord" verbally or nonverbally.

   c. How is joy a result of walking in fellowship with God? (See Galatians 5:22.)

d. List some reasons your group has to be joyful.

3. Read Nehemiah 12:44-47.

   a. What responsibilities were different people given in these verses?

   b. What contribution did all of the people make to help their spiritual leaders?

4. Describe how thanks-giving leads to thanks-living. If possible, share a specific example from your own life with the group.

DID YOU KNOW?

The Levites, mentioned 43 times in the book of Nehemiah, were descendants of Levi, one of the sons of Jacob. Though Levi himself received a negative prophecy about his future from his father, Jacob (Genesis 49:5-7), his descendants redeemed themselves on several occasions. At the golden calf incident at Mt. Sinai, the Levites stood with Moses and used their swords to wield judgment against the rebellious people (Exodus 32:25-28). The Levites were chosen by God as substitutes for the firstborn in the nation who belonged to Him (Numbers 3:11-13). Instead of an inheritance of land in Canaan, God was the Levites' inheritance (Deuteronomy 18:1-8). Since they were a "tithe" to the Lord of the tribes of Israel, they were given the tithe of Israel's resources for their support (Nehemiah 10:37; Hebrews 7:5).

Step Number 9:

DOING AWAY WITH COMPROMISE

Nehemiah 13:1-31

In this lesson we find an example of how to be relentless in rooting out sin and restoring righteousness.

OUTLINE

Because Satan is relentless in his attacks on the work of God, it is not a question of "if" the attacks will come but "when" and "how." The job of every Christian, and every local church, is to be a covenant-keeper, remembering every responsibility which lordship to Christ requires.

I. Four Violations
   A. They Forgot Their Vows of Separation
   B. They Forgot Their Vows of Support
   C. They Forgot Their Vows of the Sabbath
   D. They Forgot the Sanctity of Their Vows

II. Two Lessons
   A. Be Aware of the Craftiness of the Enemy
   B. Be Aggressive in Confronting the Enemy

Chapter 13 of Nehemiah introduces a darker theme than the steadily rising, positive theme of the chapters leading up to it. In chapter 12, we found all of Jerusalem celebrating the dedication of the wall that had been built under Nehemiah's leadership. But in the next chapter, which we will study in this lesson, we find Nehemiah absent from Jerusalem for about twelve years (verse 6). And what happens in his absence is not at all like what happened when he was present.

FOUR VIOLATIONS

While Nehemiah was in Persia, those in Jerusalem went back on four commitments they had made under his leadership.

They Forgot Their Vows of Separation

A man named Tobiah, a (half-Jew) Ammonite, had been a thorn in Nehemiah's side all during the rebuilding of the wall (Nehemiah 2:10, 19). He tried several times to undermine Nehemiah's credibility and authority with the people (6:17-19). But Nehemiah had successfully defended himself and Jerusalem against Tobiah's conspiracies to derail the rebuilding of the city.

However, when Nehemiah returned from his lengthy trip to Persia, he was shocked to find Tobiah living in one of the anterooms in the temple! A priest named Eliashib, who had become connected to Tobiah by marriage (explained below), had allowed him access to the inner sanctum of the temple, something Nehemiah never would have done (13:4-5). Tobiah had infiltrated the people of God and actually had an apartment in the temple precinct.

Nehemiah was greatly upset at Eliashib's actions and Tobiah's presence. He "threw all the household goods of Tobiah out of the room" and "commanded them to cleanse the rooms" (verses 8-9). And he restored the rooms to their original purpose as a place to store the tithes of grain, oil, and wine that were for use in temple worship.

Nehemiah might have been gone for twelve years, but he had not lost any of his zeal for the house of God. Nehemiah didn't call a meeting or ask anyone's permission. He knew defilement when he saw it and set about to make things right. He even had the rooms ceremonially purified in order to make them suitable for the work of God again (verse 9). Nehemiah would not allow spiritual wickedness to defile the work of God. He was single-minded about such things.

Tobiah's tenacity in undermining Nehemiah's work was amazing. He was as tenacious as the devil himself, and that is the lesson for us. Just when we think we've gained victory over our enemy's attempts, we find him sneaking in by another means. The Jews had forgotten what they had read in the Word of God: "No Ammonite or Moabite should ever come into the assembly of God" (verse 1). Twelve years earlier, when the Jews heard Ezra read these words, "they separated all the mixed multitude from Israel" (verse 3). But they forgot their vow. Tobiah waited until their spiritual leader was absent, and until the people had settled into their old routines, before making his move. And that is exactly how Satan will attempt to defile us.

They Forgot Their Vows of Support

The rooms Tobiah was living in were obviously not being used for their original purpose. They were empty of the "grain offerings, the frankincense, the articles, the tithes of grain, the new wine and oil" (verse 5) which were supposed to be stored there. And why were they empty? Because "the portions for the Levites had not been given them." So "each of the Levites and the singers who did the work had gone back to his field" (verse 10).

Things had completely fallen apart in Nehemiah's absence. So he called the Jewish leaders together and asked, "Why is the house of God forsaken?" And then he "set them in their place" (verse 11). Nehemiah was back!

His message to them was this: Because they stopped giving their tithes and offerings for the Levites, they created a vacuum—the rooms where the offerings should have been stored were empty. And into that vacuum—that absence of righteousness—evil went. And our hearts are like that storeroom in the temple. If God is not filling our hearts, if we have allowed a vacuum to appear, the devil will quietly move right in. The people had forgotten their vows to support the work of God with their tithes and offerings. They had forgotten to make God the priority with their material resources.

Because the resources stopped coming in, the Levites had no support, so they returned to the outlying areas to try to create a living for themselves. Nehemiah reprimanded the leaders—those who had signed a covenant agreement to be faithful to the Word of God and its stipulations (9:38) and to bring their tithes into the storehouse of the temple (10:37–39). Their last statement was, "And we will not neglect the house of our God" (10:39). They had made a vow to support the temple but had not kept it, and Nehemiah was not pleased.

So "all Judah brought the tithe of the grain and the new wine and the oil to the storehouse" (13:12).

They Forgot Their Vows of the Sabbath

The third vow the people had forgotten while Nehemiah was gone was their vow to honor the Sabbath day and keep it holy (13:15-22). Keeping the Sabbath had been part of the covenant agreement they had signed a dozen years earlier (10:31). We do not live under Jewish Sabbath laws today in the Christian Church—but they did, and they were not keeping them.

One of the reasons the Jews spent seventy years in Babylon was for violating the Sabbath year command to let the land rest every seven years (Exodus 23:10-11; Leviticus 25:4). For 490 years they ignored that law. They "owed" God seventy years of rest for the land, and He removed them from the land for seventy years to allow that to happen (Leviticus 26:34; 2 Chronicles 36:20–21). But they didn't learn how serious God was about the Sabbath rest— whether one day out of seven or one year out of seven.

Pagan vendors from the city of Tyre had moved into Jerusalem to sell their goods seven days a week (13:16), and the Jews themselves were doing all their normal work as well (13:15). Nehemiah confronted the leaders of Judah over this just as he had the other issues (verses 17-18). Then Nehemiah took charge of the gates of the city to make sure they were closed on the Sabbath-eve, shutting out the vendors. He even drove them away from setting up shop around the base of the wall outside the city. Not surprisingly, "From that time on they came no more on the Sabbath" (verse 21).

Nehemiah was zealous and jealous for the Word of God. He was the only one who seemed to remember that it was their profaning of God's laws and His Sabbath that landed the nation in Babylon, and he knew it could happen again.

They Forgot the Sanctity of Their Vows

But there was a final problem: The Jews had begun to intermarry with the pagan population (13:23-28). They had forgotten the sanctity of marriage in God's sight. This was another area to which they had committed themselves in writing (10:30).

The men had taken wives from all the surrounding pagan nations, and many of their children did not even know how to speak Hebrew (13:23-24). This violation of their standards seemed to upset Nehemiah the most: "So I contended with them and cursed them, struck some of them and pulled out their hair, and made them swear by God, saying, 'You shall not give your daughters as wives to their sons, nor take their daughters for your sons or yourselves'" (verse 25). ("Cursed" doesn't mean what it means today—swear words. Rather, it meant pronouncing God's judgment on them for violating His laws.)

Nehemiah reminded them of King Solomon's sins with foreign wives and how corrupt he became and how it cost him his throne. The Jews knew this, but were ignoring their own history. And so do many Christians today, rationalizing their decision to take a non-Christian partner in marriage, something that is a clear violation of the Word of God (2 Corinthians 6:14-18). It doesn't matter how much you pray about it and how much peace you think God has given you, that particular peace is not from Him. God will never give you peace about violating His Word.

Remember Eliashib, the priest who gave Tobiah an apartment in the temple to live in? Eliahsib's grandson had married the daughter of Sanballat who was one of Tobiah's partners in the attacks on Nehemiah (2:10). So a chief priest had allowed his grandson to marry into the family that was part of an alliance against Israel! And Nehemiah chased the offender away (verse 28).

Nehemiah had to be a brokenhearted man at this point. He was exercising great courage and determination in cleaning up the mess he had found, and he continued to pray that God would be merciful (verses 14, 22, 29). But this had to have hurt him deeply.

We can draw two important lessons from this period in Nehemiah's ministry in Jerusalem.

Two Lessons

Both lessons have to do with living with an enemy: being aware of his craftiness and being aggressive in confronting him.

Be Aware of the Craftiness of the Enemy

The enemy of God—whether Satan himself or those he empowers—will look for any opportunity to come in and oppose and disrupt the work of God.

I have read about a little mostly-Protestant town in the north of Ireland called Ballymena, in which the Christian people are fond of holding cottage prayer meetings. A Christian lady there planned for a series of prayer meetings, one each week for three weeks. Her next-door neighbor was a young Catholic woman to whom the Protestant lady had been witnessing. In fact, she invited the young woman to attend the first of the three prayer meetings. She declined the invitation, but the next morning inquired how the meeting had been. The hostess declared it to have been a lovely meeting: "We had 35 people attend and the house was full. Won't you join us next week?"

The young woman declined again, but the next week asked how the second meeting went. Again, the hostess said it was wonderful: "This time the house was full with 51 people in attendance. I hope you'll join us for the final meeting next week." But again the young woman said she'd be busy.

The third meeting came and went and the young Catholic lady inquired about the meeting. "Oh, it was wonderful!" the hostess said. "The best meeting yet. We had 62 people attending, and the cottage was full."

With a puzzled look on her face, the young Catholic woman said, "I'm curious. Each week you've said you had more people in attendance, yet each week you said the house was full. If the house was full with 35 the first week, how could it also be full with 51 and 62?"

"Oh, it's very simple," the hostess said. "We just kept moving furniture out into the yard as more people came, so the house was always full."

That little parable is a good illustration of what has to happen in our hearts to keep the enemy from finding room to sneak in. We have to keep our heart full of the Lord all the time, moving other things out to make room for Him. We can never allow a vacancy or vacuum to occur because that's when Satan will find a corner to hide in.

Are you continually keeping your heart full of the things of God? Are you removing the "furniture" of this world so as to make more room for kingdom realities? Don't leave a vacant room in your heart. You may discover a tenant has moved in without your permission.

Be Aggressive in Confronting the Enemy

Throughout the passage we are studying there are a number of action verbs indicating the energy with which Nehemiah addressed the failures of the Jews in Jerusalem. In verses 11, 17, and 25 we find the word "contended"—an aggressive word. In verses 9 and 19 the word "commanded" occurs. The word "testified" is in verses 15 and 21 (KJV). In verse 8 is the term "threw out," referring to Tobiah's furniture that Nehemiah threw out of the apartment in the temple. In verse 25 Nehemiah "cursed," "struck," and "pulled" out hair.

These are all very forceful words that describe Nehemiah's actions. He was bold and aggressive in confronting the enemies of righteousness and obedience. He didn't pray, get counsel, form committees, or the like. He saw the enemy at work and confronted those who were manifesting that work without delay.

Looking back on my years in ministry, there were probably times in the early years when I was more aggressive than I should have been. But if that was a fault, I think it's also a fault for us to become too relaxed, too tolerant, as we grow older. Sometimes we don't want to be accused of making a fuss or being too narrow-minded or intolerant, so we may let things slide that we wouldn't have when we were younger. We think, "That problem will go away if I just give it time."

But I have learned that problems don't "just go away." If we don't advance on them, they advance on us. While being aggressive against sin does not give one the right to be abusive, rude, or less than humble, the fear of offending should not be cause for holding back. There were likely more than a few people (including the guilty parties) who were offended by Nehemiah's heavy hand in restoring spiritual order in Jerusalem. But Nehemiah knew he was accountable to God (as his three prayers indicate), not to wrongdoers. When the unity and purity of God's people is being undermined and destroyed, it is time for leaders to step in and "remove the leaven" from the house of God (1 Corinthians 5:6). Sin must be aggressively arrested whether in the life of an individual or the church.

In his book on Nehemiah, *Hand Me Another Brick,* Dr. Charles Swindoll recounts the famous story of Ludwig von Beethoven's gradual descent into deafness. When he reached his fifties, and could no longer hear at all, Beethoven was reportedly seen in his house on his knees, banging his fists on the floor in frustration, as if to say, "I am going to take life by the throat. I will not quit." [1]

That is the kind of determination Nehemiah had when confronting sin in Jerusalem, and the kind of determination we must have wherever we encounter the enemies of God. The enemy is relentless, so it is not a matter of "if" there will be sin to confront, but "when." Our task is to be equipped, ready to stand firm for the sake of righteousness.

Note

1. Dr. Charles R. Swindoll, *Hand Me Another Brick* (Nashville: Thomas Nelson, 1978), 190-191.

1. Read Nehemiah 13.

   a. While Nehemiah was away, how did Eliashib and Tobiah infiltrate the temple of God? (verses 4-5)

   b. How did Nehemiah react to their actions? (verses 8-9)

   c. Why was it wrong for Tobiah to come into the assembly of God? (verse 1)

   d. Why were the rooms in the temple empty of the offerings normally stored there? (verse 10)

   e. What were Nehemiah's actions against the rulers who forgot their vows of support? (verse 11)

f. Did the people react to Nehemiah's orders? If so, what did they do? (verse 12)

g. What Jewish law did the people of Jerusalem disregard while Nehemiah was away? (verses 15-16)

h. What did Nehemiah command of the nobles? Did they listen in return? (verses 21-22)

i. In Nehemiah 10:30 the Israelites committed themselves to a marriage vow. Did they keep this vow? (verses 23-24)

j. Explain what it means in verse 25 when it says that Nehemiah "cursed" the Israelites.

2. What action verbs throughout Nehemiah 13 indicate Nehemiah's energy to address the Israelites' failures?

   a. Verses 11, 17:

   b. Verses 9, 19:

   c. Verse 25:

3. What has been your experience with making commitments to God or to others, then failing to keep them? How do you handle this when it happens?

1. Read Nehemiah 13 as a group.

   a. Where did Nehemiah go and for how long?

   b. Discuss who Tobiah was and why he was not allowed in the assembly of God.

   c. In what way did one sin lead to another sin in this situation?

   d. Give an example of how one sin can lead to another sin today.

   e. What did Nehemiah command to be done in verse 9?

   f. What question did Nehemiah ask the rulers in verse 11?

g. What did Nehemiah ask of God in verse 14?

h. In what ways were the Israelites no longer observing the Sabbath? (verse 15-17)

i. What changes did Nehemiah institute in order to make sure the Israelites observed the Sabbath again? (verses 19-22)

j. Who did Nehemiah use as an example for why the Israelites were not to marry people from pagan nations? (verse 26)

2. What is the first lesson we can learn from this chapter in Nehemiah?

a. Why should we always be on guard against Satan?

b. How can we make sure we do not leave a vacancy in our life for the enemy to sneak into?

3. Discuss the importance of being aggressive in confronting the enemy, Satan.

   a. Why is confronting sin more important than worrying about offending people?

   b. Is it possible to confront the sins of others aggressively and loving? Why or why not?

DID YOU KNOW?

Tobiah was an Ammonite who fell under the prohibition of Deuteronomy 23:3-6 that no Ammonite or Moabite should ever enter the assembly of the Lord. The Moabites and Ammonites were the incestuous sons of Lot, Moab and Ben-Ammi, birthed by his two daughters (Genesis 19:36-38). They were the perpetual enemies of the descendants of the sons of Jacob and sought to have the prophet Balaam curse the Israelites on their way to the Promised Land (Numbers 22:4–24:25). Because Israel was related to the Ammonites through Lot, the nephew of Abraham, they were forbidden from attacking the Ammonites (Deuteronomy 2:19). But the Ammonites never hesitated to attack Israel, even after the captivity, through Tobiah. Ezekiel predicted their ultimate destruction, which happened in the intertestamental period (Ezekiel 25:1-7).

Step Number 10:

BECOMING SEPARATE UNTO THE LORD

Selected Scriptures

In this lesson we survey the life and leadership legacy of Nehemiah.

OUTLINE

Ideas are cheap while burdens can be expensive. Ideas can be discarded but burdens have to be seen through. Nehemiah didn't have an idea to rebuild the wall around Jerusalem, he had a burden. And it was that burden that revealed the life and leadership traits for which he is known.

I. Three Important Things About Nehemiah
    A. Nehemiah's Ordination

    B. Nehemiah's Organization

    C. Nehemiah's Opposition

II. Five Important Things About Leadership
    A. Nehemiah Was a Man of Prayer

    B. Nehemiah Was a Man of Purpose

    C. Nehemiah Was a Man of Persuasion

    D. Nehemiah Was a Man of Perspective

    E. Nehemiah Was a Man of Persistence

Wilbur Chapman relates this story about a group of mountain climbers in the Swiss Alps. They were making rapid progress one day until suddenly one of them slipped. Since they were all tied together those ahead of the one who was falling were jerked backward and were sliding down as well. It seemed that the entire chain of climbers would go over the cliff together.

But the guide, at the head of the line, saw what was happening. In a split second he slammed his ice pick deep into the ice and held on. When the falling chain of climbers jerked against him he hung on to his ice pick—and stopped the falling motion of the others. All who were connected by rope to the guide were saved.

Chapman said that Nehemiah was like that guide. He was Israel's stay. He was like a mountain guide who safely held the climbers together who were about to fall away. Looking back through the history of the Old Testament, had there not been a man by the name of Nehemiah, it is hard to say what would have become of God's people.

As we conclude this study on ten steps to spiritual renewal, it's appropriate to summarize what we have seen in the man Nehemiah and what we can learn from him.

THREE IMPORTANT THINGS ABOUT NEHEMIAH

Leadership always involves three dynamics: ordination, organization, and opposition.

Nehemiah's Ordination

Before going to Jerusalem, Nehemiah was cupbearer to the king of Persia in Susa. His own brother, Hanani, came from Jerusalem to Susa and reported to Nehemiah on the state of affairs in Jerusalem. The people were in great distress, the wall around Jerusalem had been knocked down, and the gates had been burned (Nehemiah 1:1-3).

Upon hearing this news, Nehemiah "sat down and wept, and mourned for many days" (verse 4). He prayed a brokenhearted prayer to God, confessing the sins of his people and asking for favor with the king of Persia (verses 5-11). The king noticed some time later that Nehemiah was downcast and inquired why. Nehemiah was risking his life in this situation since it was a capital offense to be downcast in the presence of the king. But Nehemiah explained to the king what he had learned about the fate of his city and the Jewish people.

God answered Nehemiah's prayer for favor as the king said, "What do you request?" (2:4) And before the day ended Nehemiah was given everything he needed to return to Jerusalem and try to save Jerusalem. He was given letters with the king's seal that gave him safe passage to Jerusalem and the right to collect the materials that would be needed to rebuild the wall. That's one of the reasons the wall was rebuilt in 52 days (6:15). Nehemiah's prayer, plea, and plan resulted in the king's permission to go.

Nehemiah's Organization

When we get to the end of Nehemiah 2, we begin to see Nehemiah's gift of organization at work. Part of the image of God in every person is to be organized, but some have a gift at being able to pull people and projects together. And Nehemiah was one of those people.

One of the first things he did upon arriving at Jerusalem, before revealing his plan to rebuild the walls, was to inspect the destroyed city and gain a perspective on what it would take to accomplish the task (2:11-16). Nehemiah was not impulsive. He was a planner who took things a step at a time. He knew he needed to give God time to help him understand the need and how to meet it. There is a great danger in arriving in a new situation and beginning to arrange the future before taking time to understand the past and the present. Nehemiah didn't make that mistake.

In chapter 2:17-20, we have his words to the people—some of my favorite in all the book. It would have been easy for Nehemiah to be overwhelmed by what he saw on his tour of the city, to bring back a doom-and-gloom report like the spies that returned to Kadesh Barnea from their reconnaissance tour of Canaan (Numbers 13-14). But his words were simple and purposeful: "You see the distress that we are in, how Jerusalem lies waste, and its gates are burned with fire. Come and let us build the wall of Jerusalem, that we may no longer be a reproach (2:17). And the people said, "Let us rise up and build" (2:18).

Whether there was a time lapse between the end of chapter 2 and beginning of chapter 3 is hard to tell, but I tend to think there was not. The high priest, Eliashib, along with other priests, "rose up" and rebuilt the Sheep Gate—and others joined them (3:1-32). The work seems to have begun immediately.

Nehemiah's Opposition

But as is always the case when the work of God goes forward and begins to change lives and the world, there was opposition against Nehemiah—from within and without the city.

1. Opposition From Without

The opposition from outside the Israelite community (4:1-9) came from Tobiah, an Ammonite, and Sanballat, a Samaritan. Both had become influential in the region in the absence of the Israelites and did not welcome Nehemiah's efforts to rebuild the city. They used all kinds of derision and sarcasm among the people to try to make Nehemiah look foolish. Nehemiah prayed that God would deal with them (4:4-5) and kept on building.

When derision didn't work, Sanballat and Tobiah tried delay—they recruited Arabs, Ammonites, and men from Ashdod to help them stir up trouble against Jerusalem (4:7-9). Troublemakers against God will always find allies. Satan will make them readily available whenever the work of God is going forward.

Nehemiah did the only two things he could do (4:9). First, he prayed to God. Nehemiah was nothing if not a man committed to living in dependence upon God. We don't know if that's why God chose Nehemiah for this task, but if it was, it is certainly understandable. Second, after asking God to do His part, Nehemiah did his part: He "set a watch against [the enemies] day and night." He did the same two things that Jesus instructed the disciples to do in the Garden of Gethsemane: watch and pray (Matthew 26:41).

When derision and delay didn't work, Nehemiah's enemies resorted to deceit (6:1-4). They tried four different times to entice Nehemiah out of the city to "meet together." But Nehemiah knew it was a trap, that they planned "to do [him] harm." So he refused to leave the city and meet with them. God gave Nehemiah wisdom and discernment to see the danger that lay outside the city walls. So just as derision and delay had failed, so deceit failed to keep Nehemiah from accomplishing his purpose.

Satan will use every scheme (Ephesians 6:11) imaginable to undermine our efforts to obey and serve God. But God has provided spiritual armor for our protection and the presence of the Holy Spirit for direction. We need not succumb to Satan's devices.

2. Opposition From Within

If the opposition Nehemiah faced from outside the camp was serious—and it was—it was not as serious as the opposition he faced from within. As hard as it is to believe, some of the strongest opposition to the work of God will often come from the people of God.

Nothing is more discouraging to a leader than to have opposition arise from within the ranks of those he is leading, those who should be on board with what God wants to do. Opposition from the world is expected and is not as demoralizing. But when God's own people begin to slow down the work, it is heartbreaking for a leader.

When Sanballat and Tobiah were strategizing against Nehemiah, the people began to grow discouraged with the enormity of the task (4:10) and the threat of an attack (4:11). But Nehemiah went on the offensive and strengthened the guard. If you can imagine, "with one hand they worked at construction, and with the other held a weapon" (4:17)! Nehemiah was an amazing leader to get people to work in such conditions: "Do not be afraid of them. Remember the Lord, great and awesome, and fight for your brethren, your sons, your daughters, your wives, and your houses" (4:14).

The rubble was piled high and the rumors of attack were flying (4:10-11)—and that's all it took. There was never an actual attack, but just the rumor of an attack—"enemy soldiers are creeping up and hiding in the rubble within an easy arrow's shot of the Israelite workers"—was enough to deflate the Jews' spirits.

Discouragement in chapter 4 was followed by dissatisfaction in chapter 5. The very people Nehemiah was leading began to express dissatisfaction with their situation exactly as their forefathers had done with Moses in the desert on the way to the Promised Land. The people who had been captives in Egypt complained against the one who set them free. And the people who had been captives in Persia were complaining against the one who was establishing them in their homeland. Any time we take our eyes off the target—whether the Promised Land for the Hebrew slaves or a rebuilt city for the Jews with Nehemiah—we find room and reason to complain.

I have noticed that it is rarely the people who are working the hardest who voice dissatisfaction. It is those who are hanging around the periphery, doing the least amount of work, who find reasons to be unhappy. Instead of focusing on the wall, Nehemiah had to deal with the rulers and nobles among them charging the poor usurious rates of interest on money loaned to buy food and fields. So Nehemiah "became very angry," gave the situation "serious thought," and "rebuked the nobles and rulers" (5:6-7). And the practices were stopped. Nehemiah the leader solved another crisis—and the wall was completed in 52 days (6:15).

FIVE IMPORTANT THINGS ABOUT LEADERSHIP

I have identified five aspects of Nehemiah's leadership style that are easily transferable to godly leaders today.

Nehemiah Was a Man of Prayer

Godly leadership does not exist without prayer. Nehemiah was a godly man and a godly leader; therefore, he was a man of prayer. I believe it is true throughout biblical history as well as Church history that the men and women God has used have always been those who were committed to prayer. It is impossible to sustain the vision and weather the vicissitudes of leadership apart from the strength, encouragement, and guidance received through prayer.

Prayer is the common denominator of leadership because godly leadership is not based on human strength or initiative. Godly leaders are accomplishing God-sized tasks—supernatural and supra-human tasks—and they can only be accomplished in the strength God provides. Throughout the book that bears his name we find Nehemiah praying—sometimes short prayers, sometimes long prayers, but always praying.

Nehemiah Was a Man of Purpose

Nehemiah knew what he was supposed to do. He was not confused in the least about his mission: rebuild the wall and hang the gates of Jerusalem to give the people of Israel a sense of security and hope for the future.

Steven Covey, author of *The Seven Habits of Highly Effective People,* says the most important thing a leader can do is write out his own personal mission statement. At seminars he conducts for leaders, he teaches them how to create such a personal mission statement. Sometimes it takes hours, even days, to sit alone and deliberate until that mission becomes clear. But when it does, there is a new sense of purpose that accompanies it, a new set of marching orders. A purpose statement allows us to say "Yes" to the right things and "No" to the wrong things.

Do you have a personal mission statement? Do you know why God has called you to Himself and what it is He has equipped you to accomplish in this life for Him? Without such a vision, life becomes a process of maintaining the status quo instead of reaching for new horizons. Days and weeks can become years, and years a lifetime, without any particular sense of accomplishment.

That was not true of Nehemiah. He was a man who lived his life on purpose.

Nehemiah Was a Man of Persuasion

Most leaders are persuasive people—when they look over their shoulder in life, they discover there are people following them. *Persuasive* doesn't mean "salesman." It means helping people clarify a godly purpose, helping them paint a picture of the future, helping them see that it's possible to accomplish something they want to do but didn't think they could. And Nehemiah was that kind of leader. He was able to motivate a group of discouraged people to pick up their tools and weapons and rebuild a city wall under the threat of attack from within and without. He helped people see the same thing that another godly leader helped the people of His day see: "With men this is impossible, but with God all things are possible" (Matthew 19:26).

Nehemiah Was a Man of Perspective

When Nehemiah heard from his brother how Jerusalem was in ruins, he began to think and deliberate. Three days after arriving in Jerusalem, he went around the city at night inspecting the broken-down walls before announcing his intention. In both cases he was gaining perspective. Nehemiah seems to have been the kind of leader who was able to envision how something could be done. He had a picture in his mind's eye of how people and purpose could unite to undertake and complete a project.

The opposite of perspective is impulsiveness—coming upon a need and jumping to a conclusion about what ought to be done before taking the time to gain perspective. The problem with that approach is doing the wrong things, or perhaps doing the right things in the wrong order or wrong way. Perspective is often gained through prayer: "Lord, what would You have me do. Please give me wisdom and guidance." We've already said Nehemiah was a man of prayer. It's no surprise that he was also a man of perspective.

Nehemiah Was a Man of Persistence

Finally, Nehemiah was a man of persistence. To be honest, I would not have wanted to be a man trying to derail Nehemiah. As far as we know from the book of Nehemiah, this man was unstoppable. He was single-minded when it came to rebuilding the wall around Jerusalem and was not going to allow anyone to keep that from happening. And he succeeded, completing the wall around Jerusalem in an amazing 52 days!

The key to persistence is the belief that "He who calls you is faithful, who also will do it" (1 Thessalonians 5:24). Until God says, "Quit," our task is to continue until the project is complete.

1. What are the three dynamics that leadership always involves?

2. Read Nehemiah 1:1-11; 2:1-10.

   a. When Nehemiah heard that the wall around Jerusalem had been knocked down, how did he handle the news? (Nehemiah 1:4)

   b. For what reason was Nehemiah able to rebuild the wall in only 52 days? (Nehemiah 2:4-9)

3. Read Nehemiah 2:11-18.

   a. In what way did Nehemiah begin to plan the rebuilding of the wall? (verses 11-16)

   b. What did Nehemiah and his followers do once he saw the distress of the city? (verse 18)

   c. As believers, why do you think it is so necessary to be organized in the work of God?

4. Read Nehemiah 4:1-17.

   a. Where did opposition come from outside of the Israelite community? (verses 1-3)

b. As is often the case, what was the only thing Nehemiah could do against his enemies? (verse 9)

c. Why do you think the need for prayerfulness among leaders is so crucial?

d. Where did opposition come from within the Israelite community? (verses 10-11)

e. Why can a leader who is trusting in the Lord be confident in the face of obstacles and changes in direction?

5. Describe the five aspects of Nehemiah's leadership that are listed below.

   a. Prayer:

   b. Purpose:

   c. Persuasion:

   d. Perspective:

   e. Persistence:

6. Why is it important for Christian leaders to demonstrate these aspects as they lead?

GROUP QUESTIONS

1. Read Nehemiah 2:11-20.

   a. Why did Nehemiah take his time after he arrived in Jerusalem before revealing his plan to rebuild the wall?

   b. How did Nehemiah encourage the people to begin rebuilding the wall? (verses 17-18)

   c. How is the work of rebuilding the wall described in verse 18?

2. Read Nehemiah 4:7-23; 6:1-4.

   a. What was Nehemiah's first response to the opposition he faced?

   b. How else did Nehemiah respond to the opposition that came from outside the Israelite community? (verses 9-23)

3. How did the discouragement of the Israelites in chapter 4 lead to their dissatisfaction with their situation in chapter 5?

4. Why does godly leadership require prayer?

5. Discuss the importance of having a personal mission statement.

    a. If you have a personal mission statement already, share it with the group.

    b. How does having a mission statement help you accomplish more for Christ?

6. What actions of Nehemiah indicate that he was a man of perspective?

7. Why is it important to have perspective and not act impulsively as a leader?

8. Read 1 Thessalonians 5:24 together. How does this verse encourage you to continue to persevere in serving God no matter the circumstances? If comfortable, share your answer with the group.

DID YOU KNOW?

B oth Nehemiah's name and his father's name, Hacaliah (Nehemiah 1:1) end in the Hebrew suffix *yah*, short for Yahweh. It may indicate that his family was loyal and conservative, faithful to the tenets of Judaism. Nehemiah was the cupbearer to the Persian king Artaxerxes I, a position of high honor and responsibility in that day. Cupbearers were responsible for tasting the king's food and drink to make sure it was not poisoned. Cupbearers are mentioned during Joseph's tenure in Egypt (Genesis 40:1, NIV) and during the reign of Solomon in Israel (1 Kings 10:5). Nehemiah lived with the burden of Jerusalem for four months before discussing it with the king: from the month of Kislev (November–December; Nehemiah 1:1) to Nisan (March–April; Nehemiah 2:1).

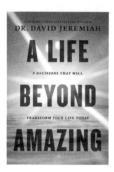
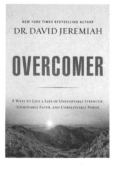

EVERYTHING YOU NEED

God never intended for us to stumble our way through the course of each day and journey into our future unprepared. He has given us everything we need to walk confidently through life! In *Everything You Need: 8 Essential Steps to a Life of Confidence in the Promises of God*, Dr. Jeremiah examines the words of 2 Peter 1 and shows us how to add diligence, virtue, knowledge, self-control, perseverance, godliness, brotherly kindness, and love to our faith.

FORWARD

Many of us want our life to make a difference, but we aren't sure how to go about accomplishing that goal. Too often, life's circumstances can weigh us down and prevent us from living the life we desire. In *Forward* Dr. Jeremiah will take you through Scripture and teach you how to discover God's purpose for your life and then to move forward in it. God has a plan for your life!

Each of these resources was created from a teaching series by Dr. David Jeremiah. Contact Turning Point for more information about correlating materials.

For pricing information and ordering, contact us at

P.O. Box 3838
San Diego, CA 92163
(800) 947-1993
www.DavidJeremiah.org